Thank you for being our valued customer. We are so grateful for the trust you have placed in us.

This coloring book has 56 unique pretty mandala designs. Alternate pages are left blank to prevent bleed through.

We sincerely hope you are satisfied with your purchase and enjoy coloring these pretty mandalas!

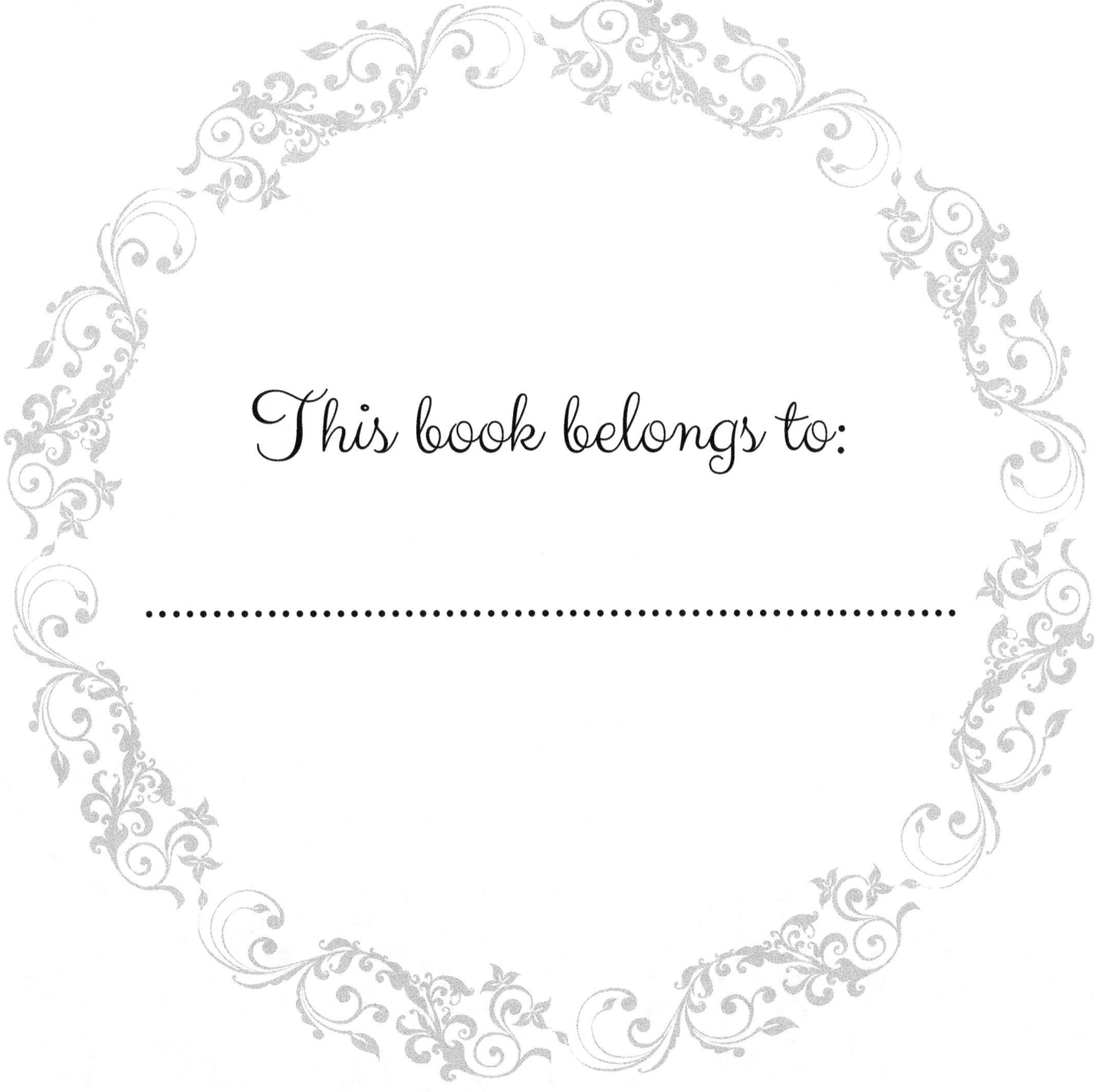

This book belongs to:

....

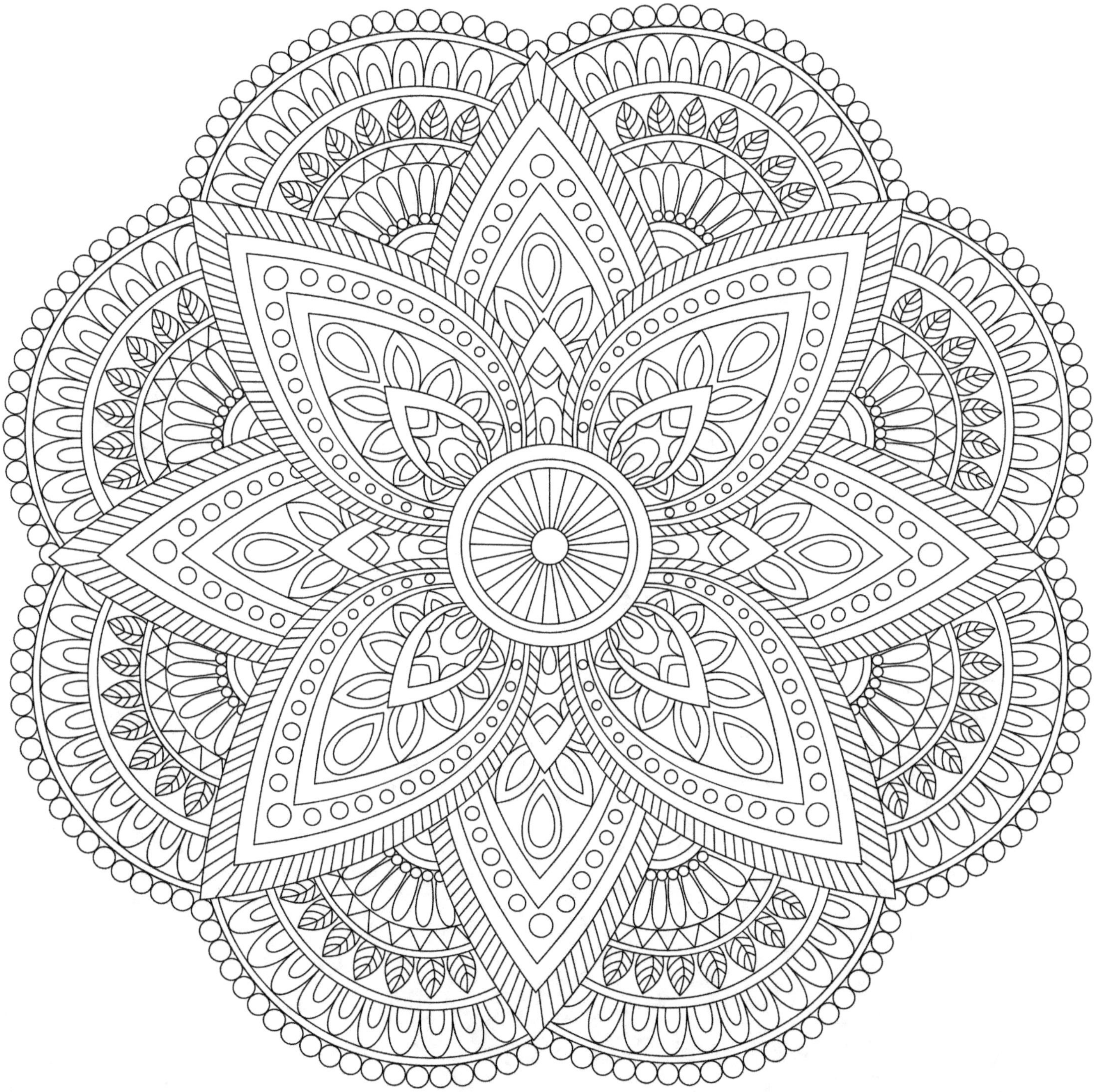

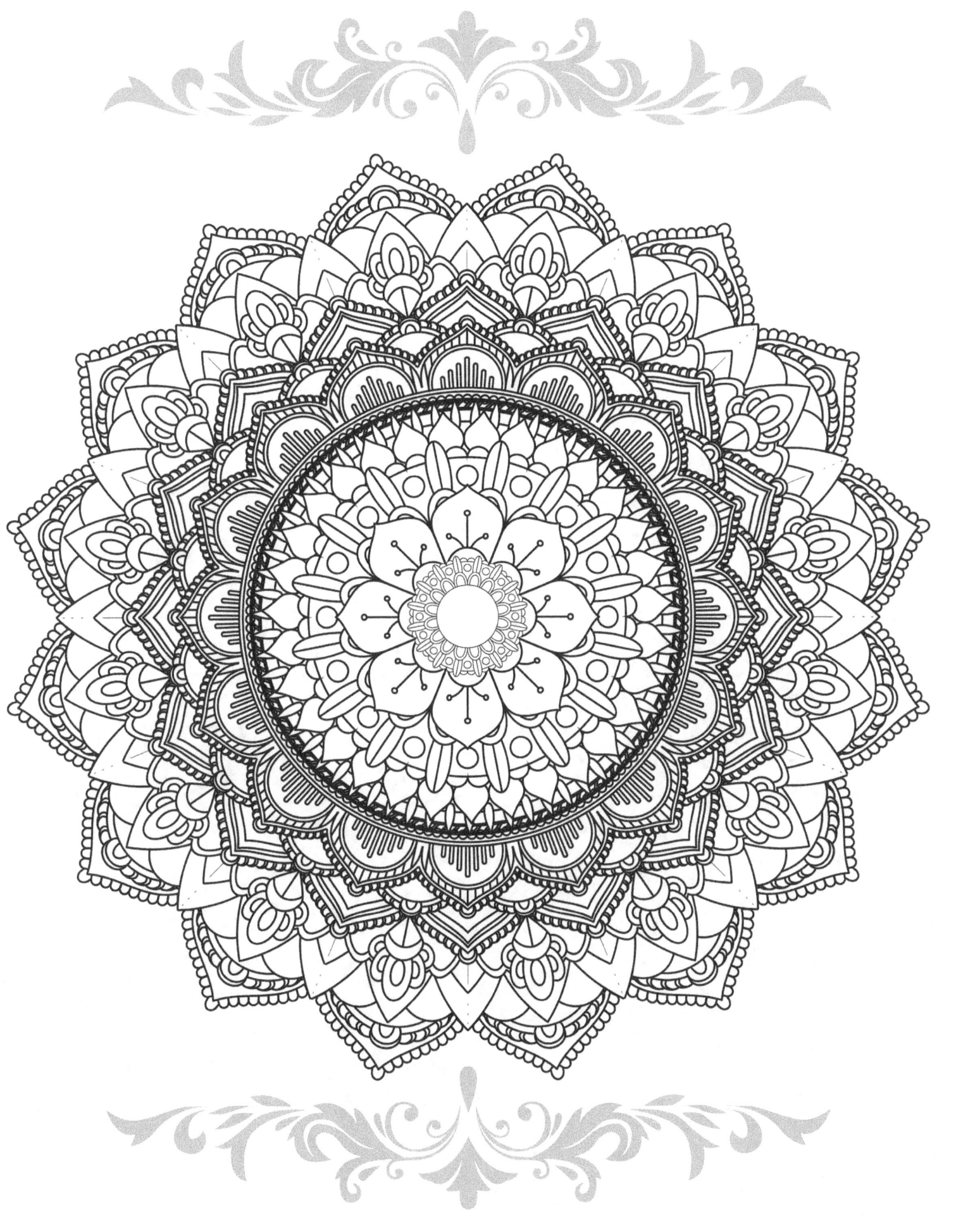

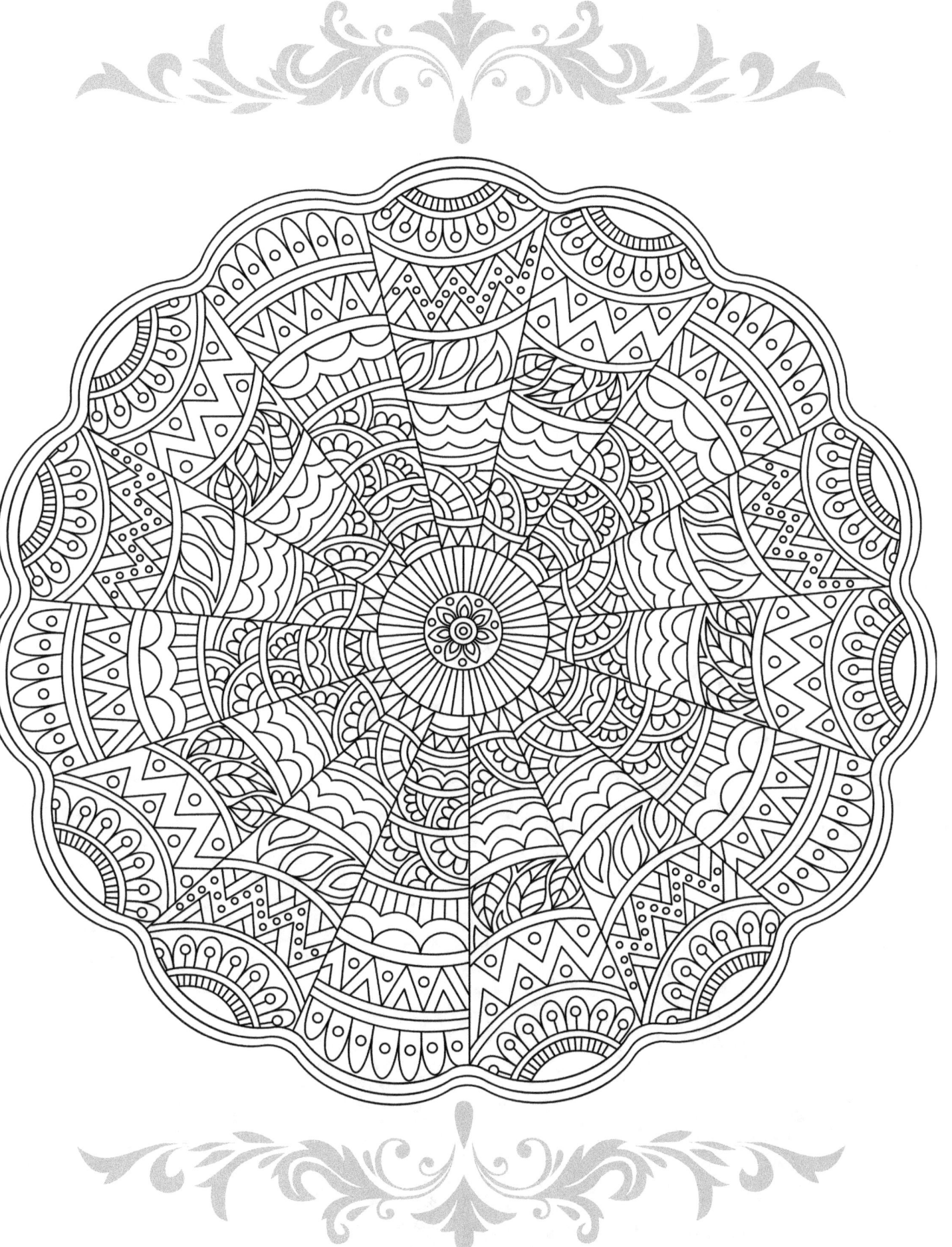

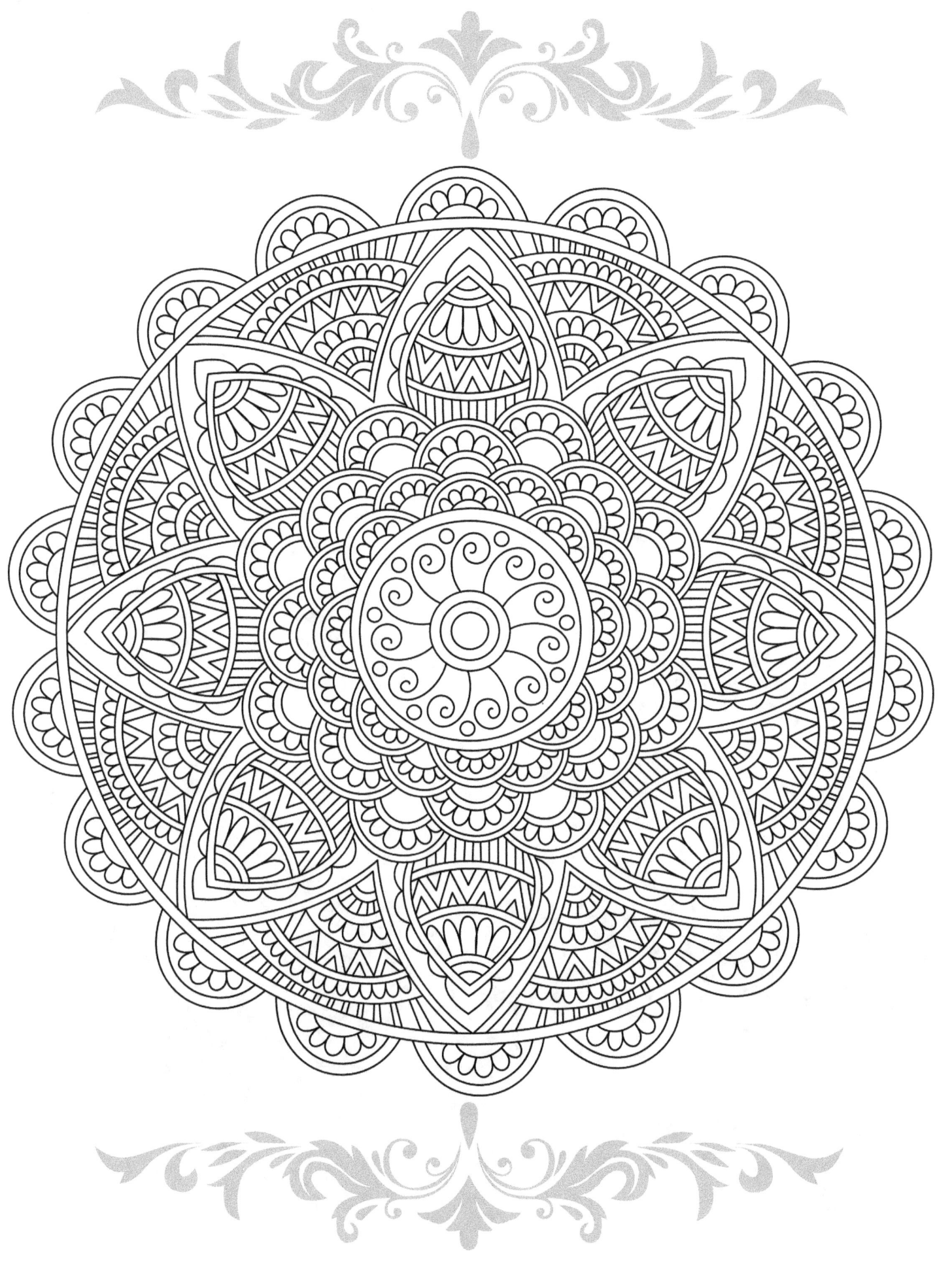

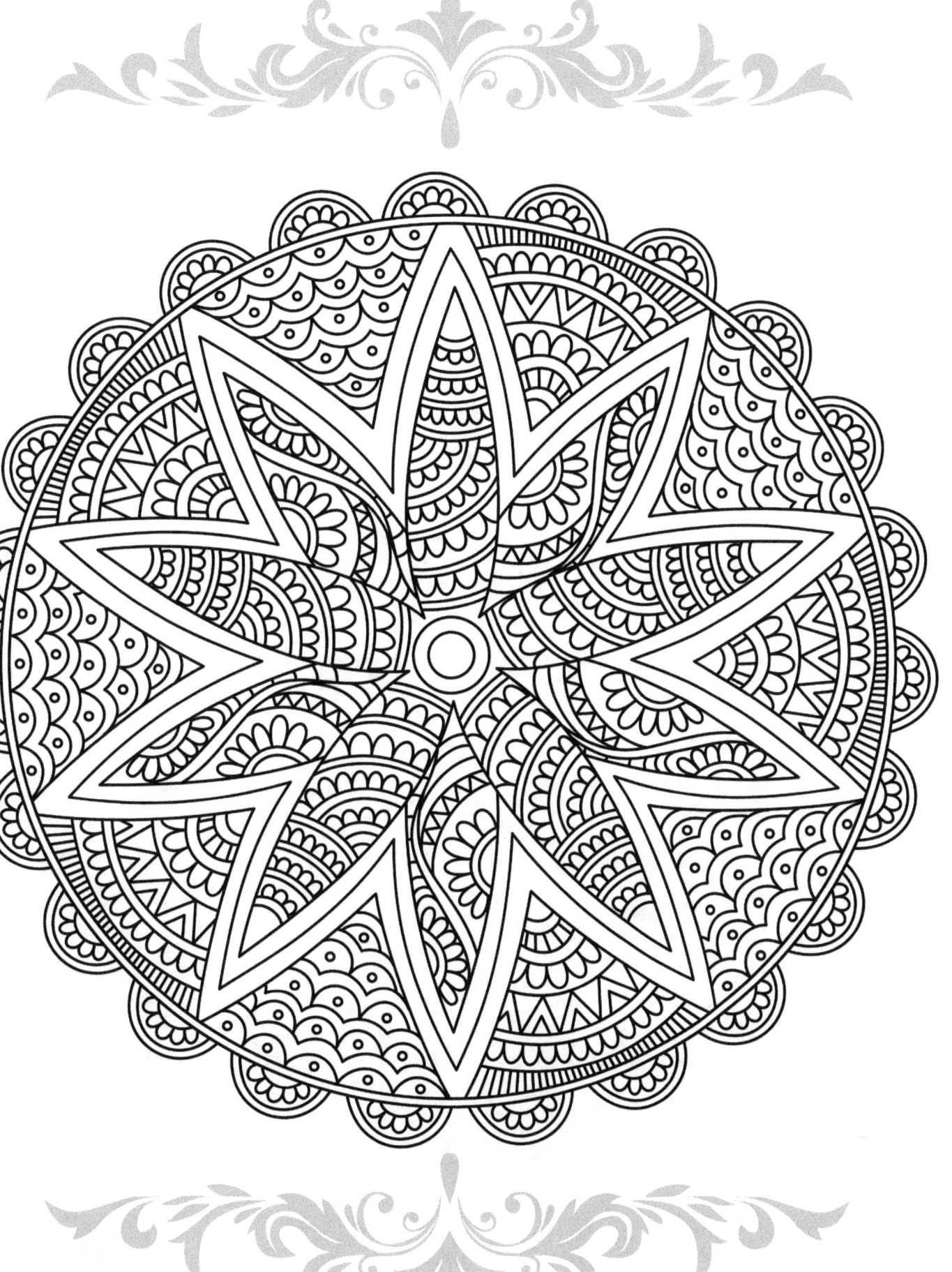

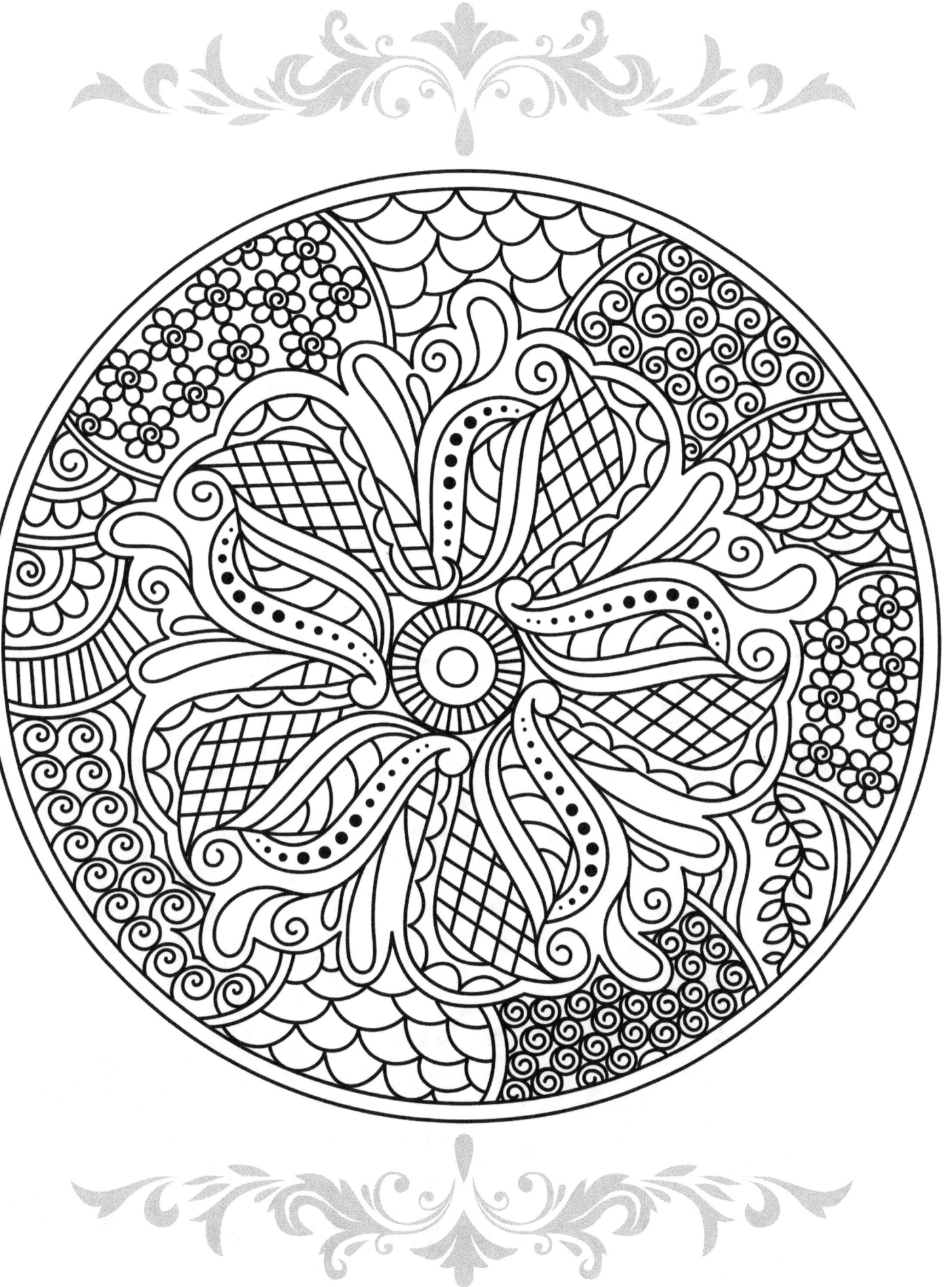

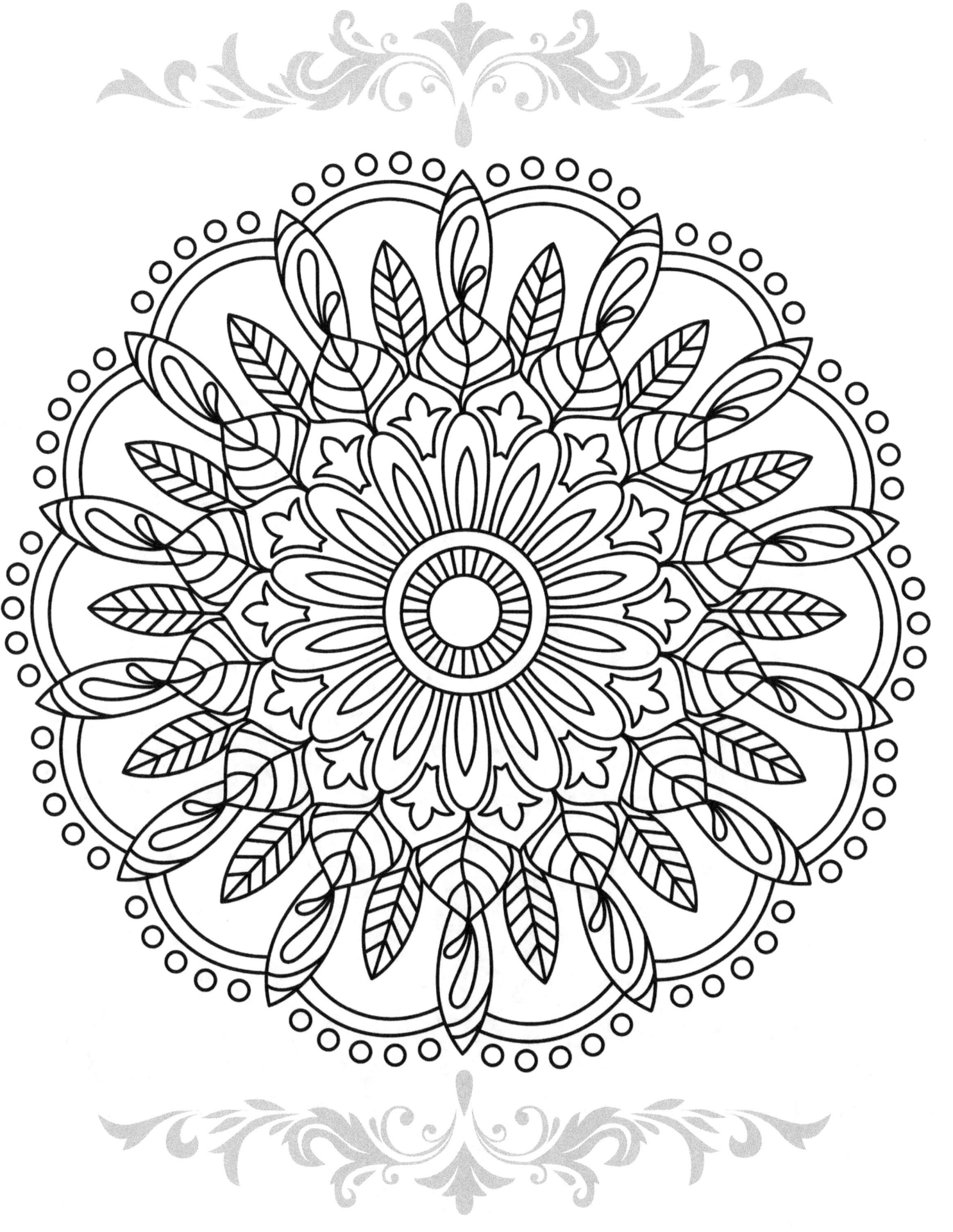

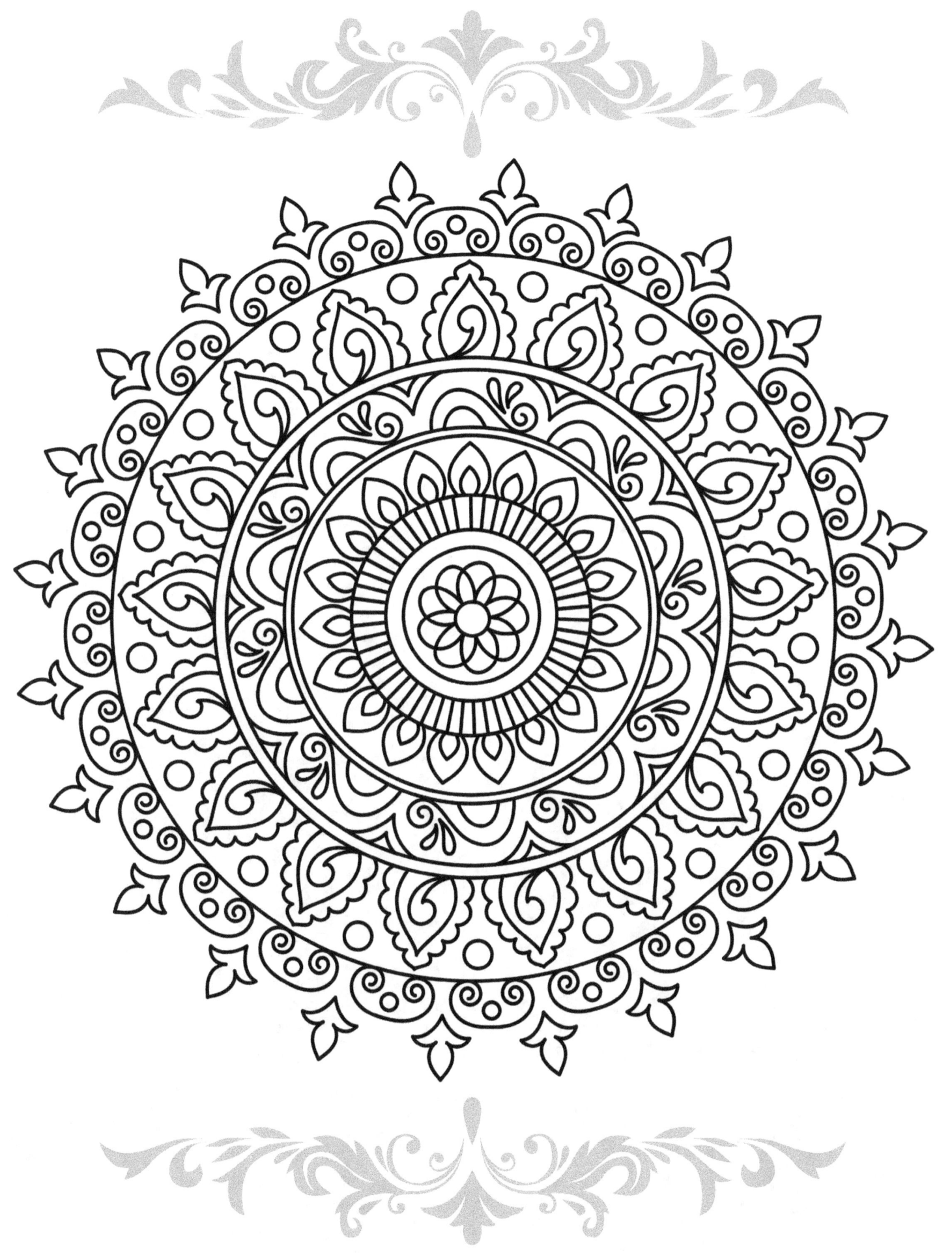

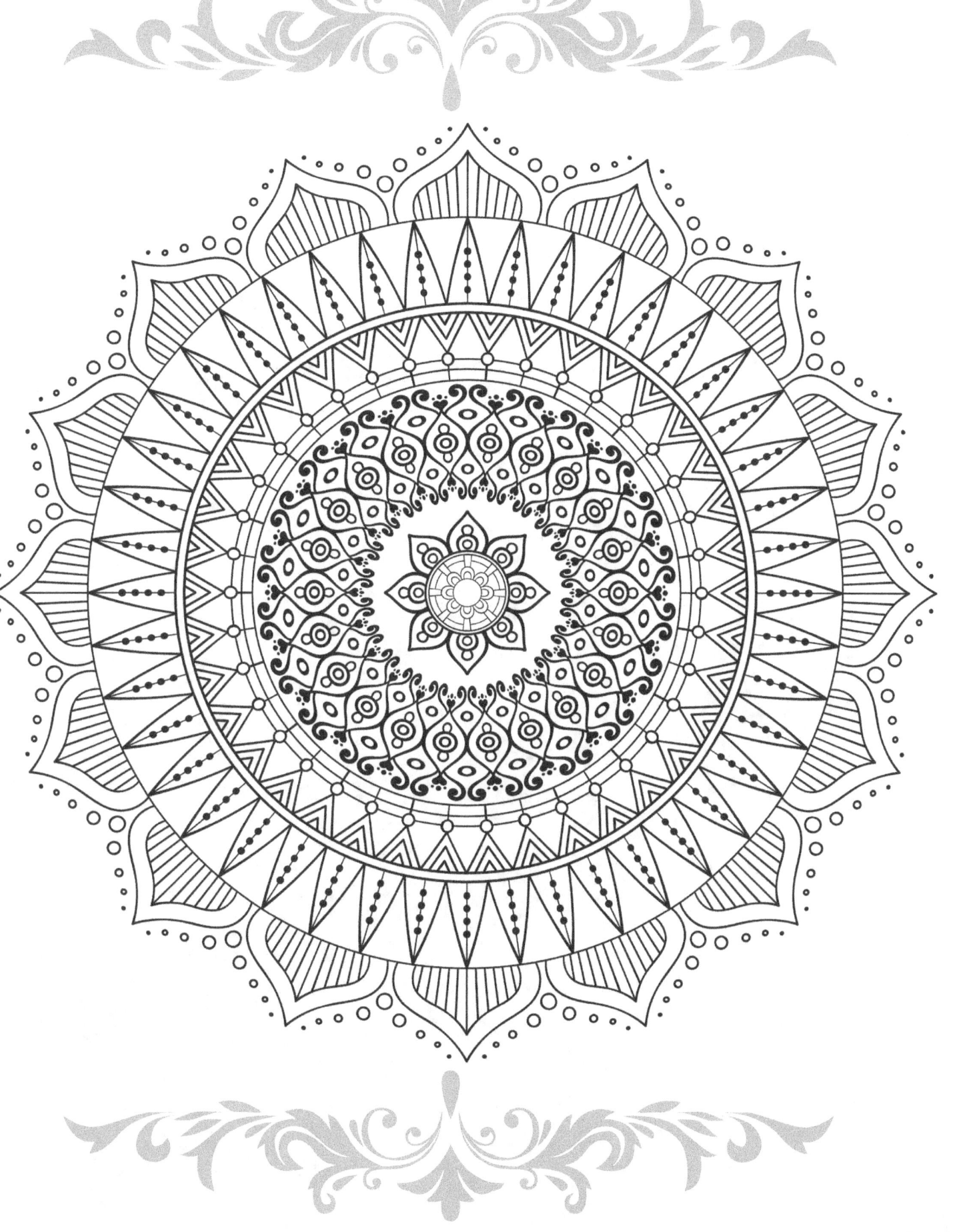

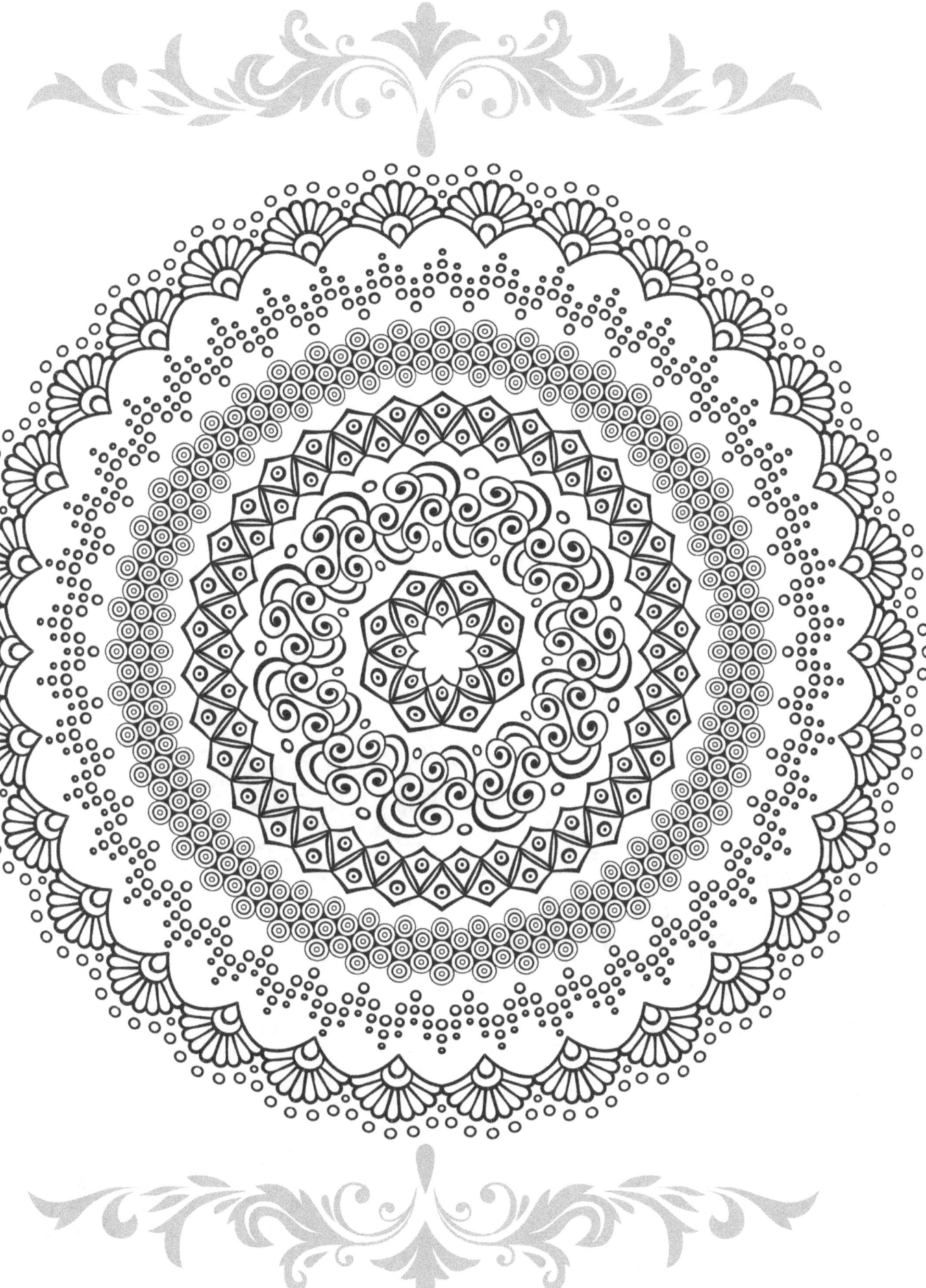

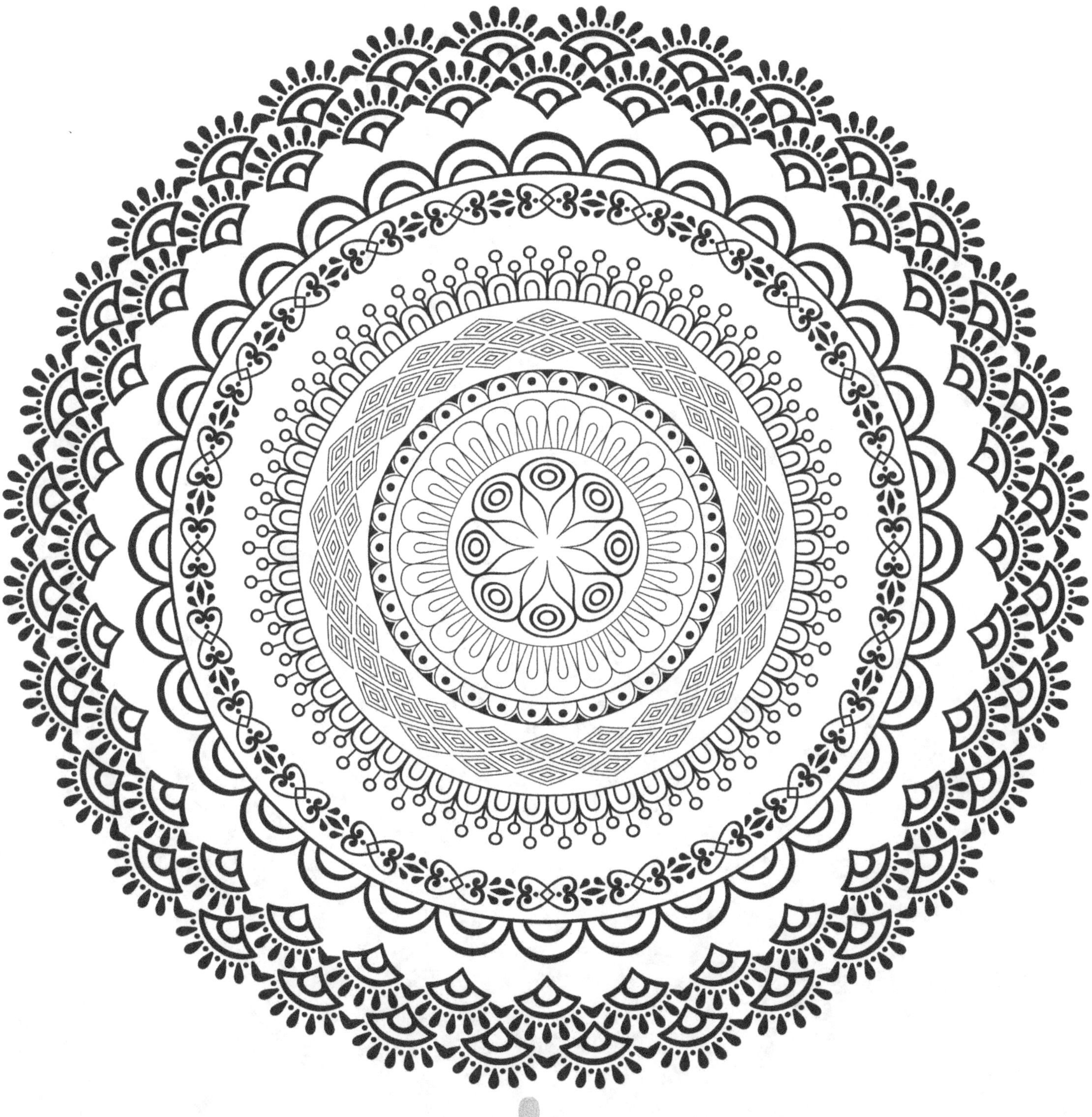

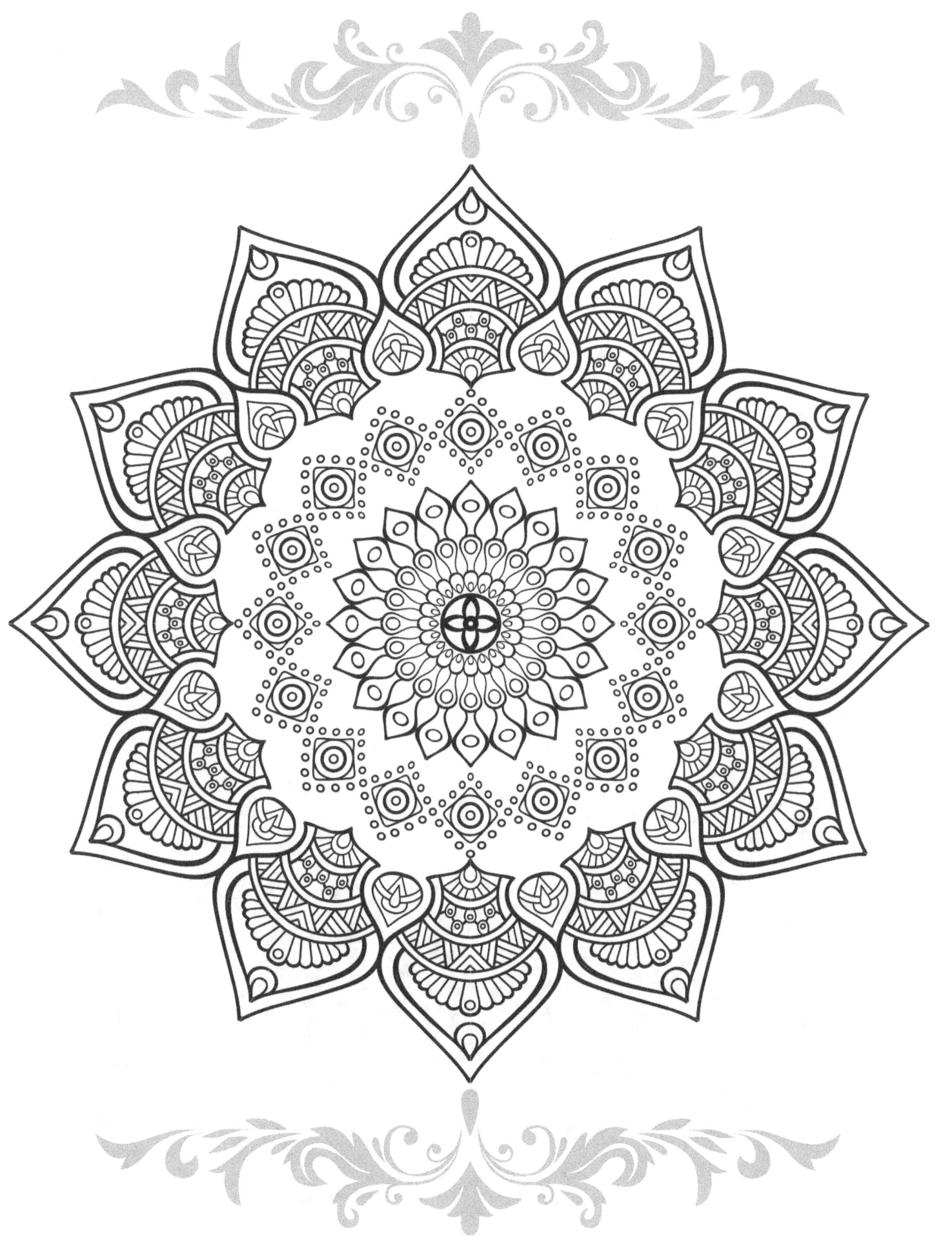

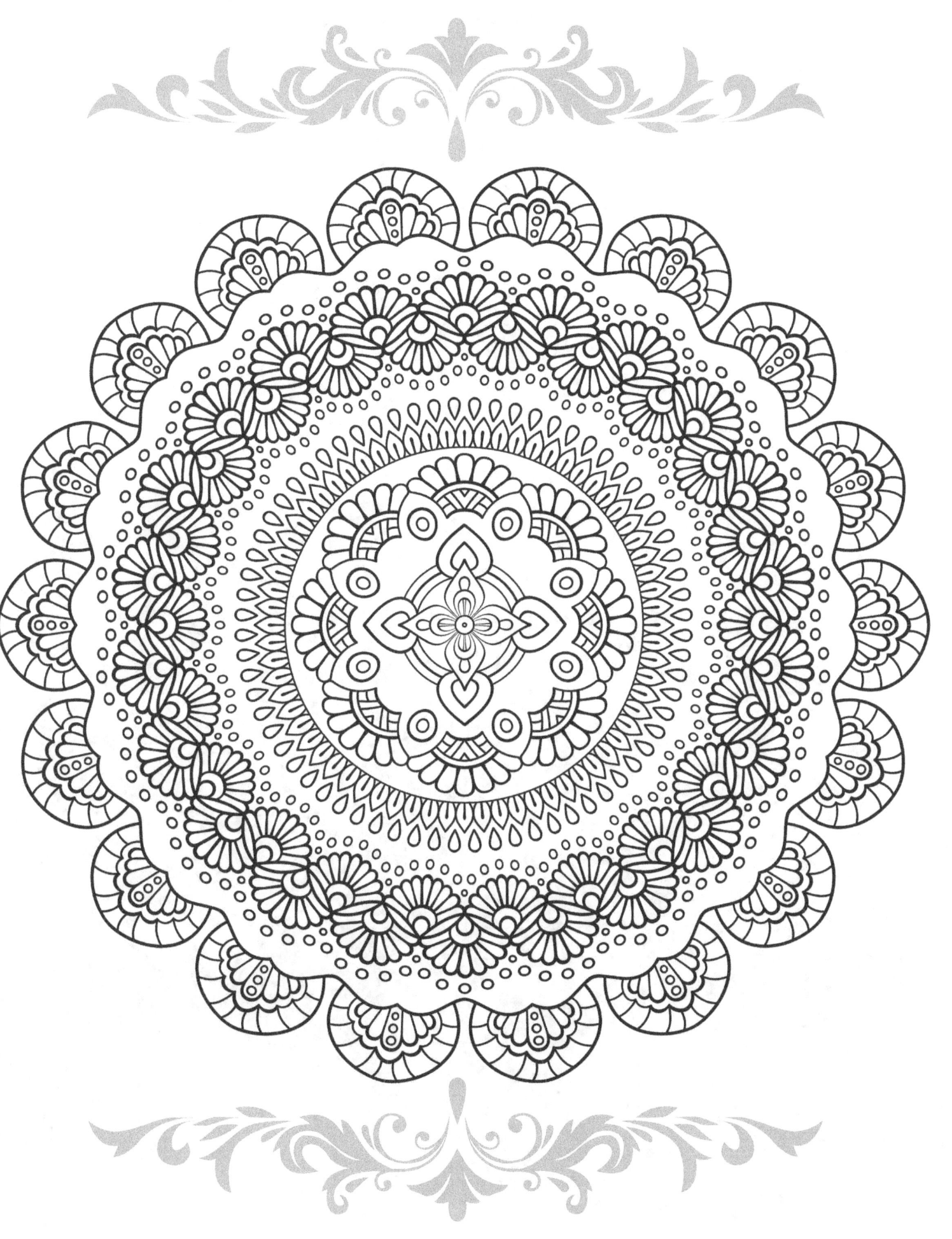

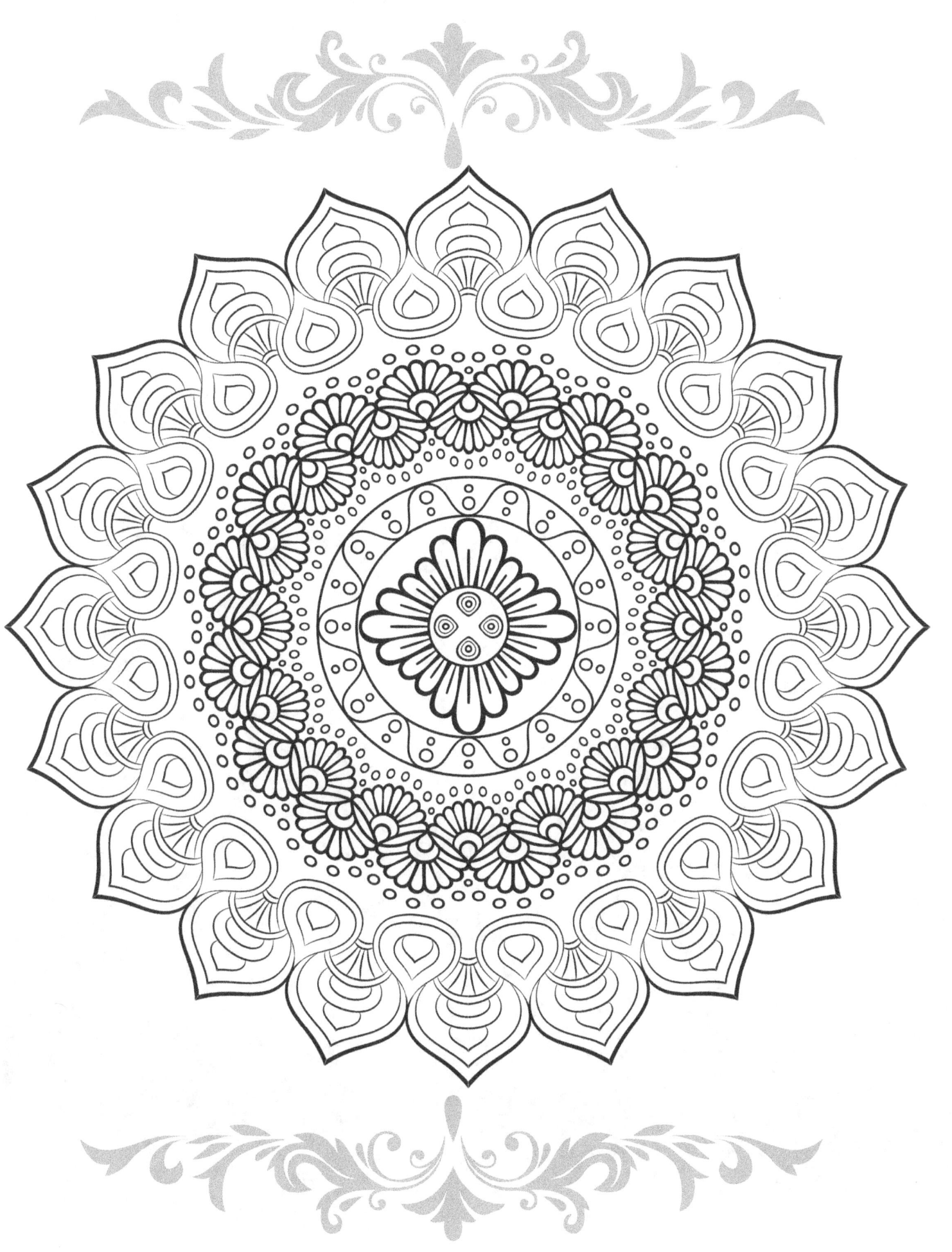

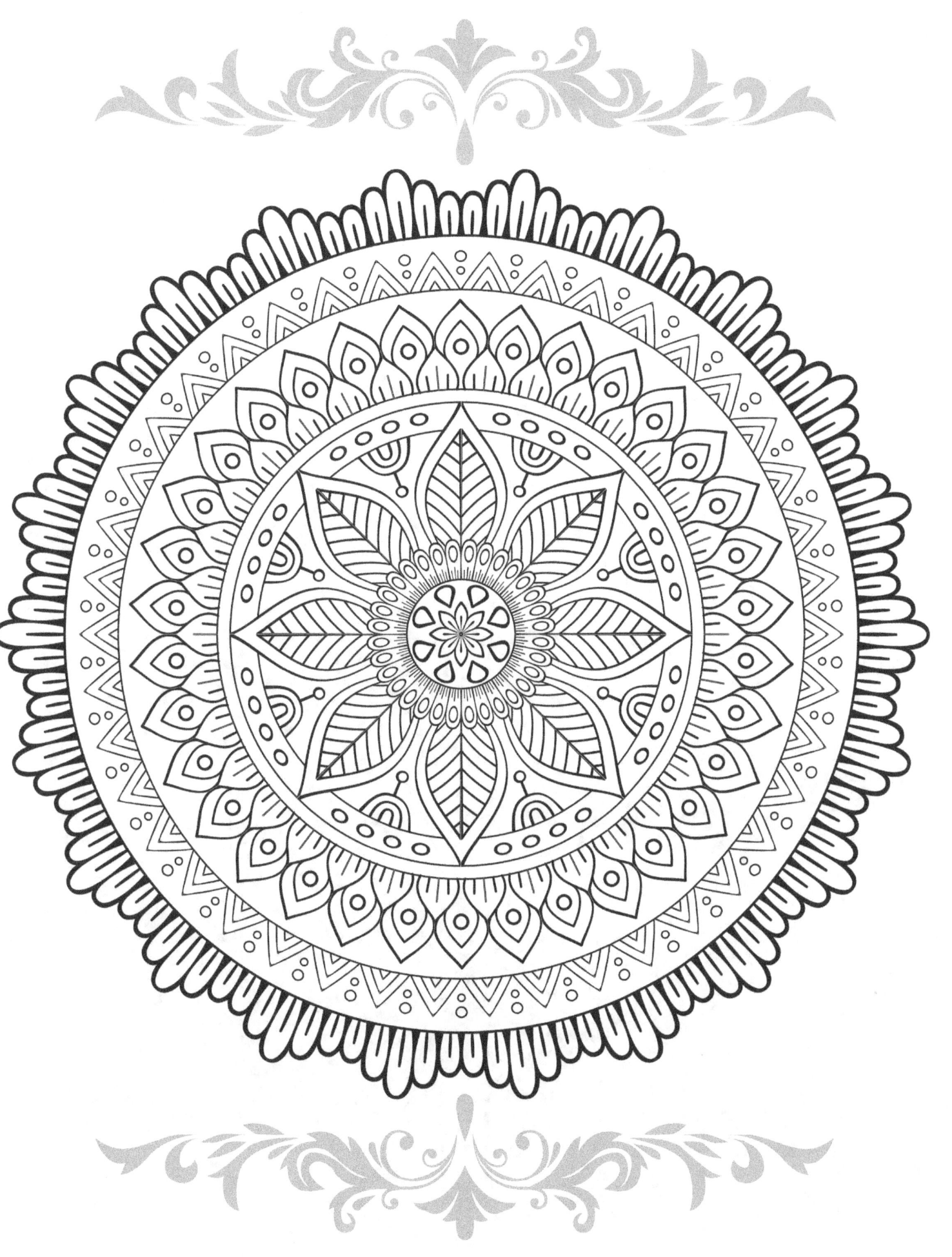

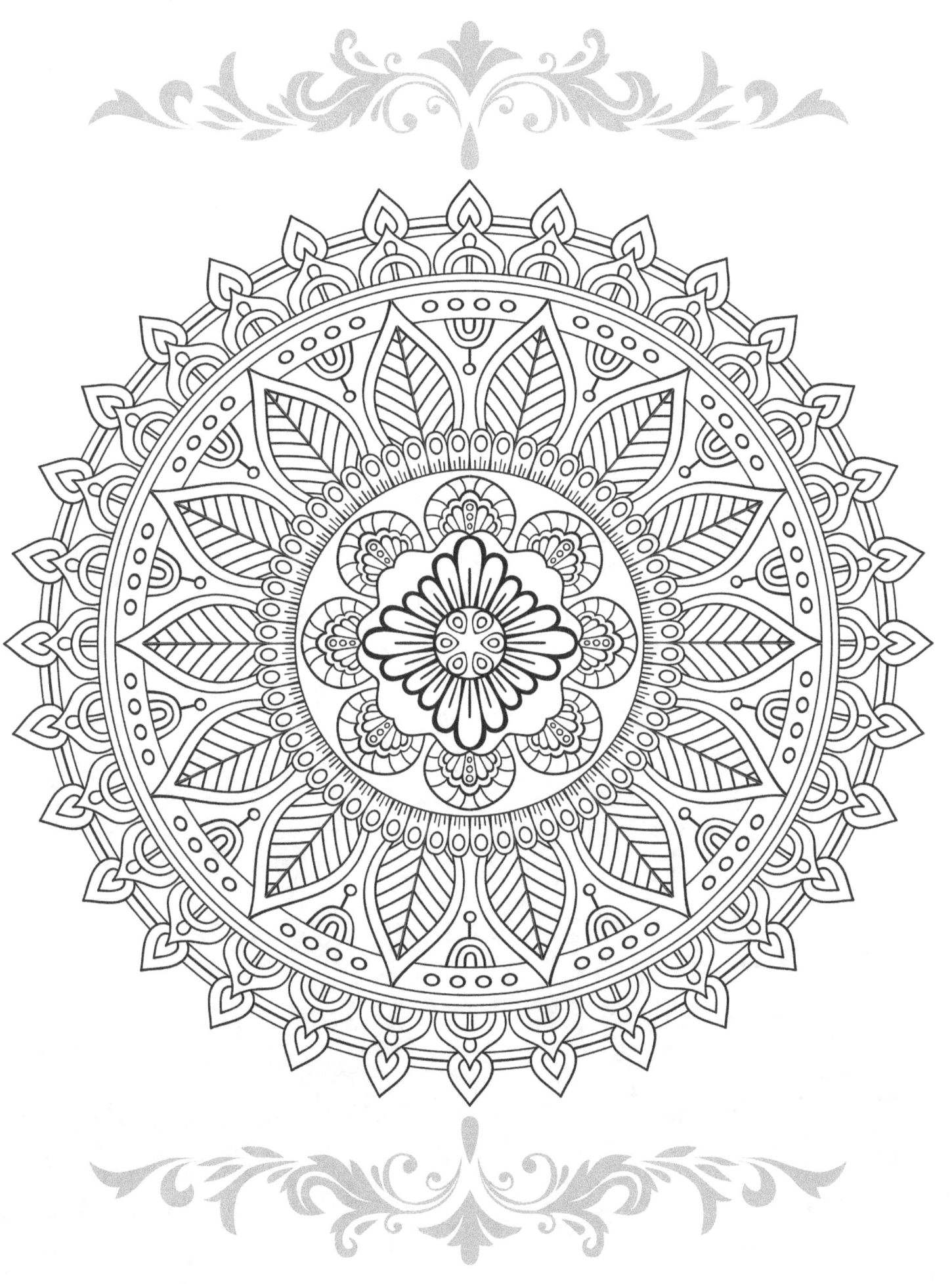

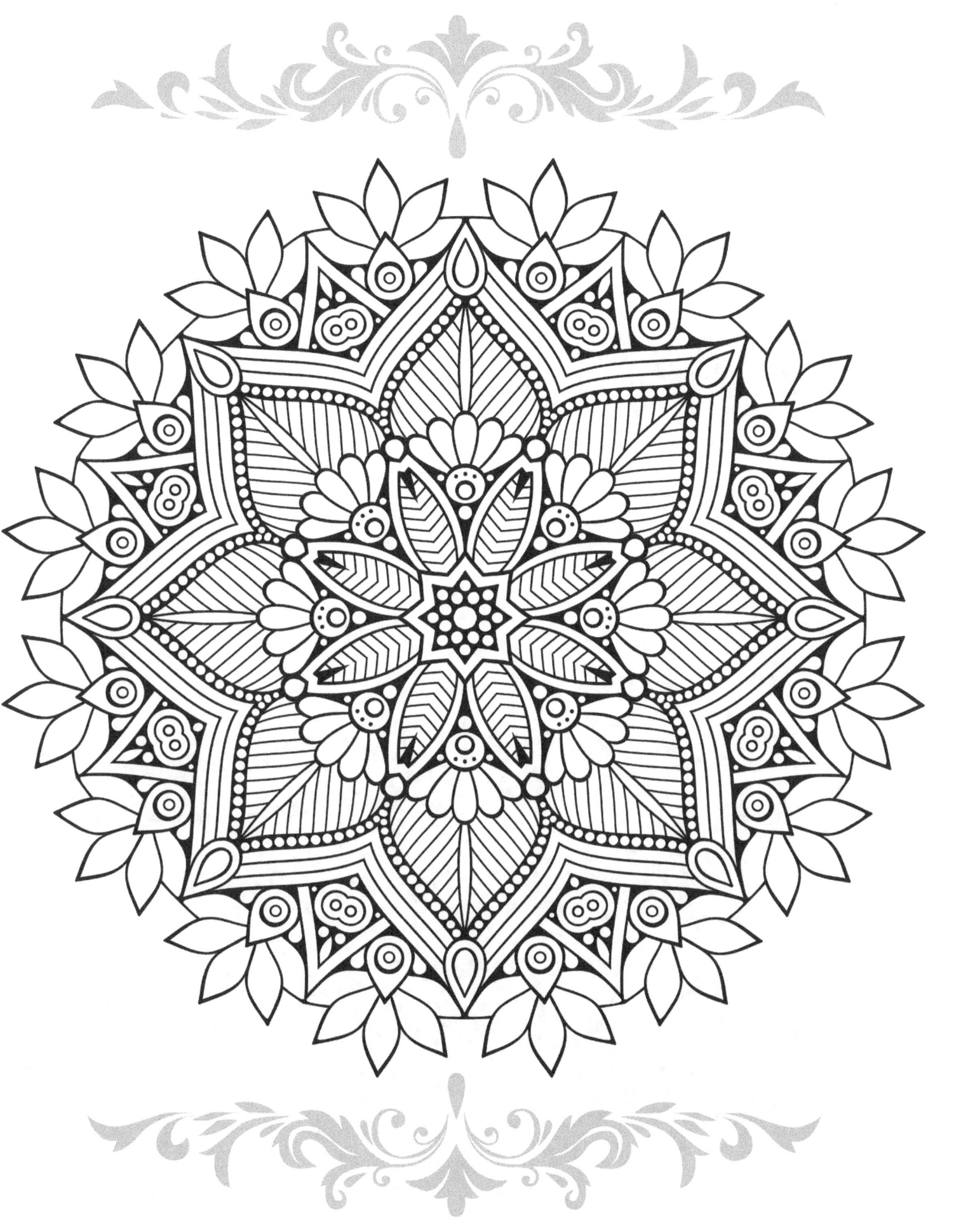

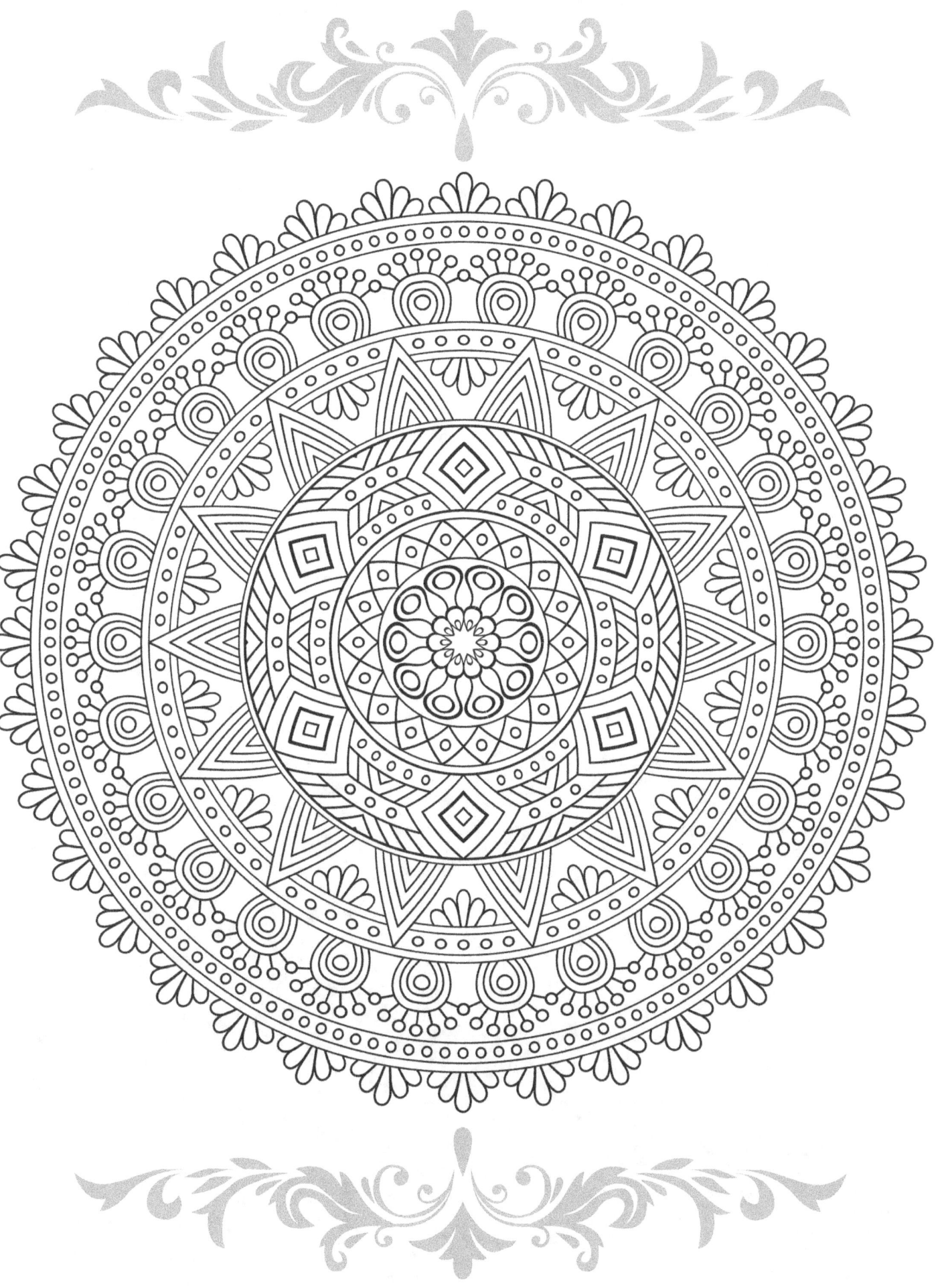

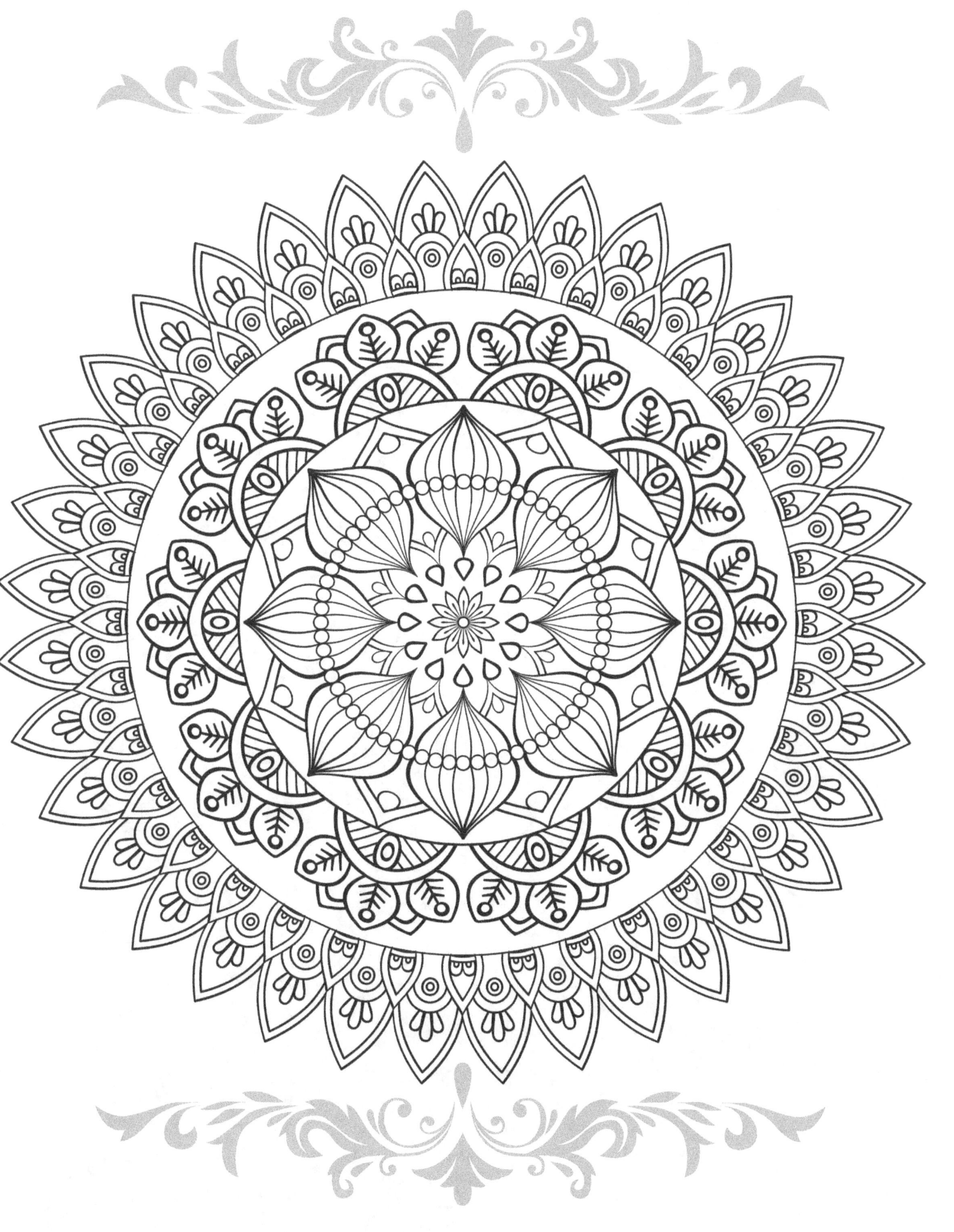

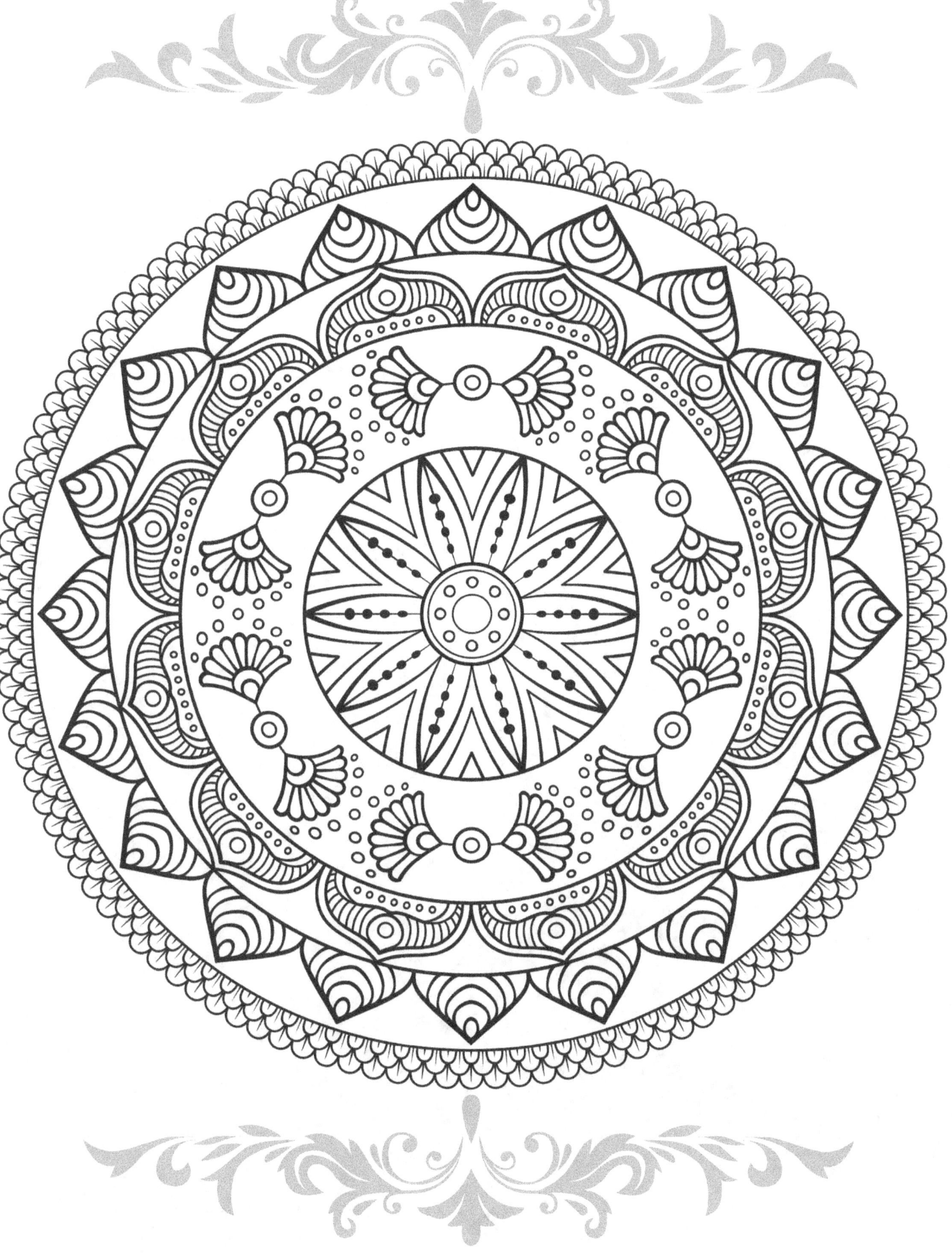

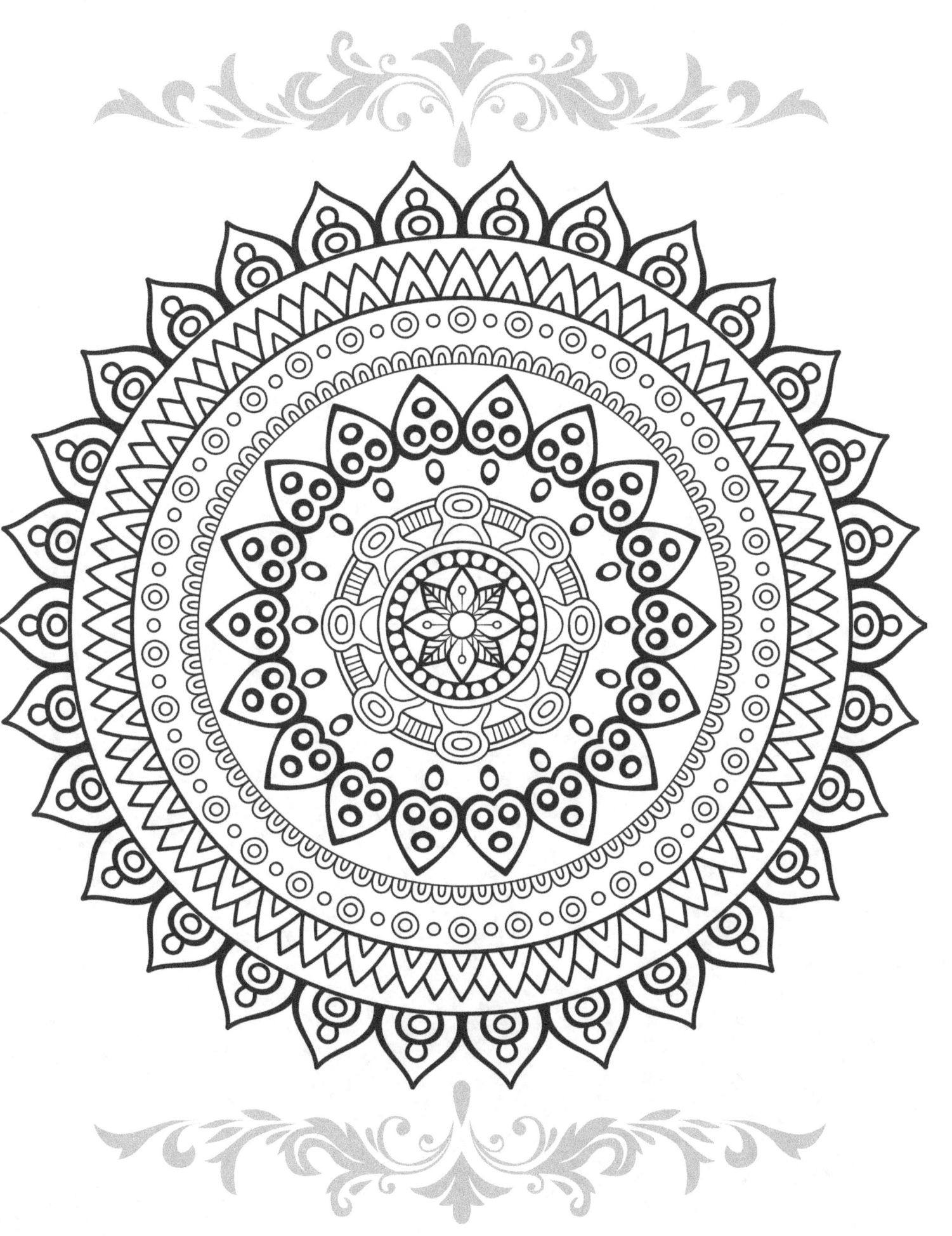

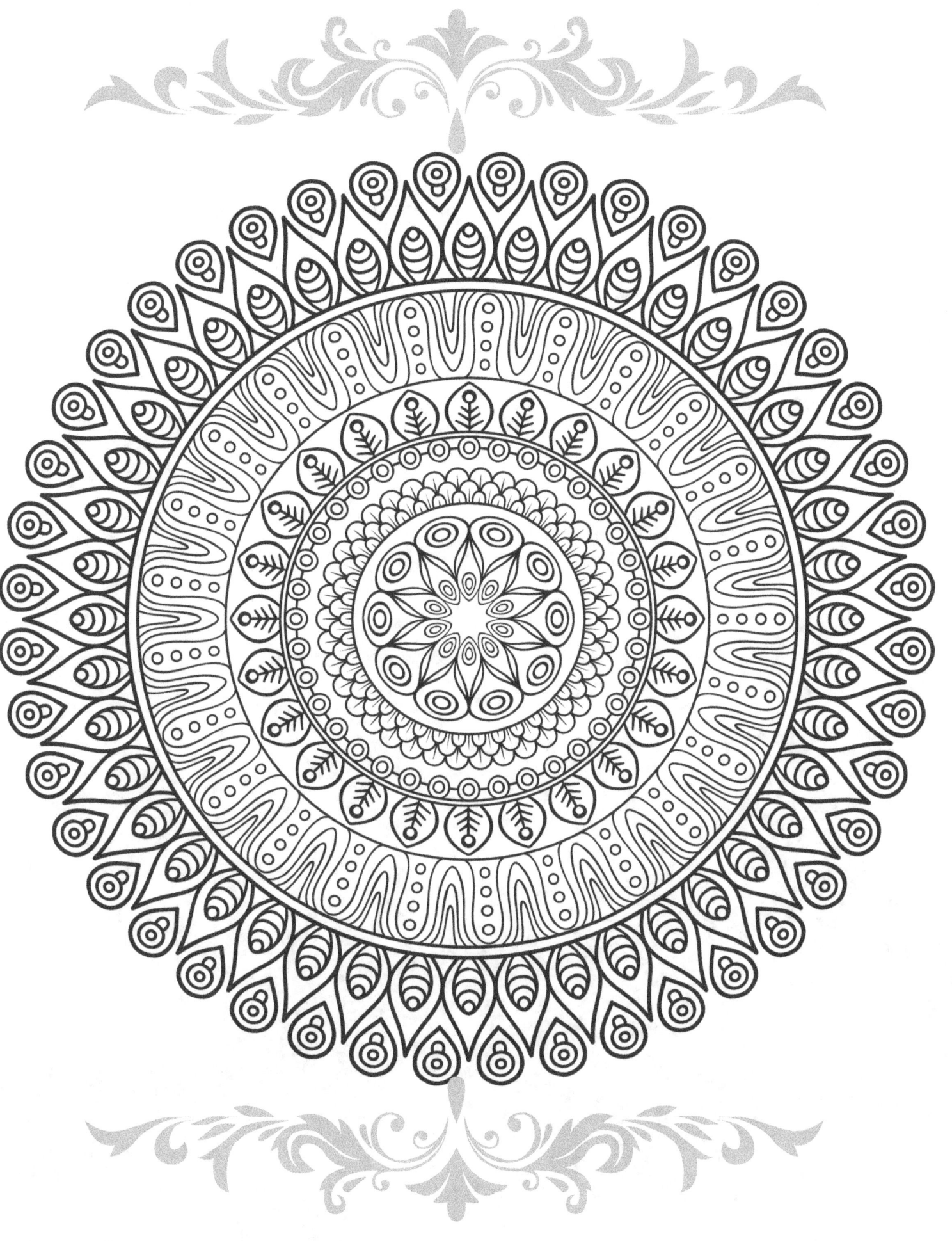

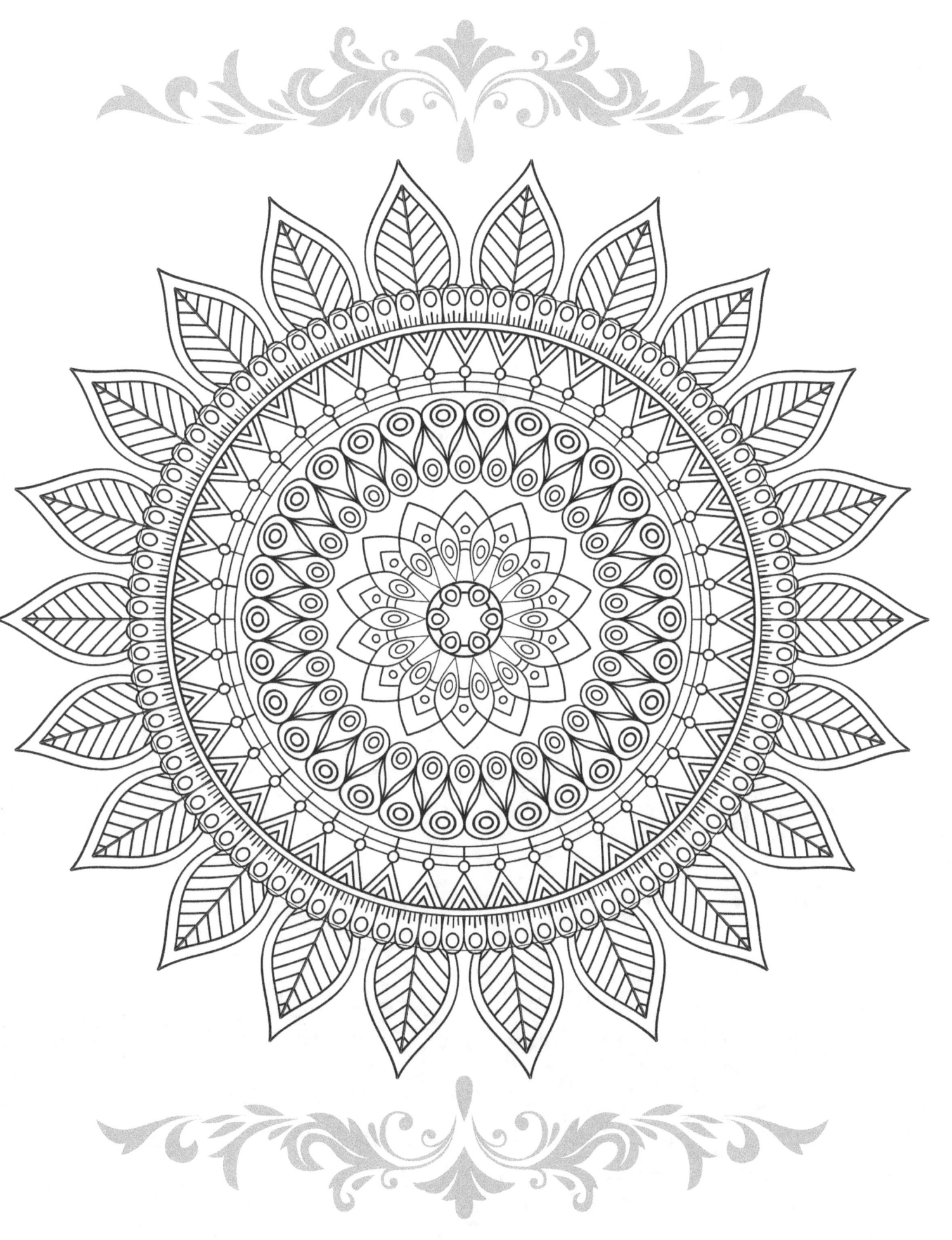

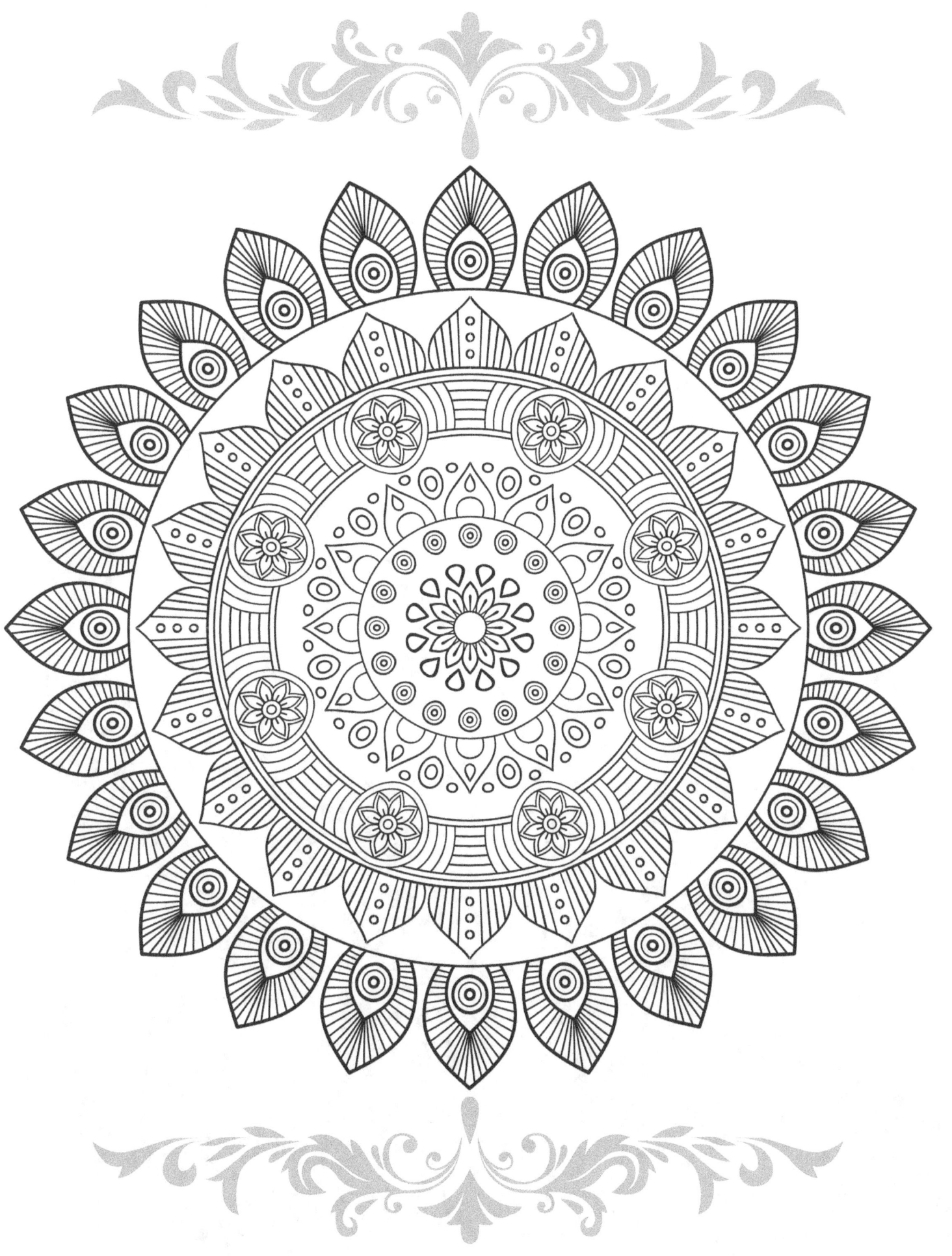

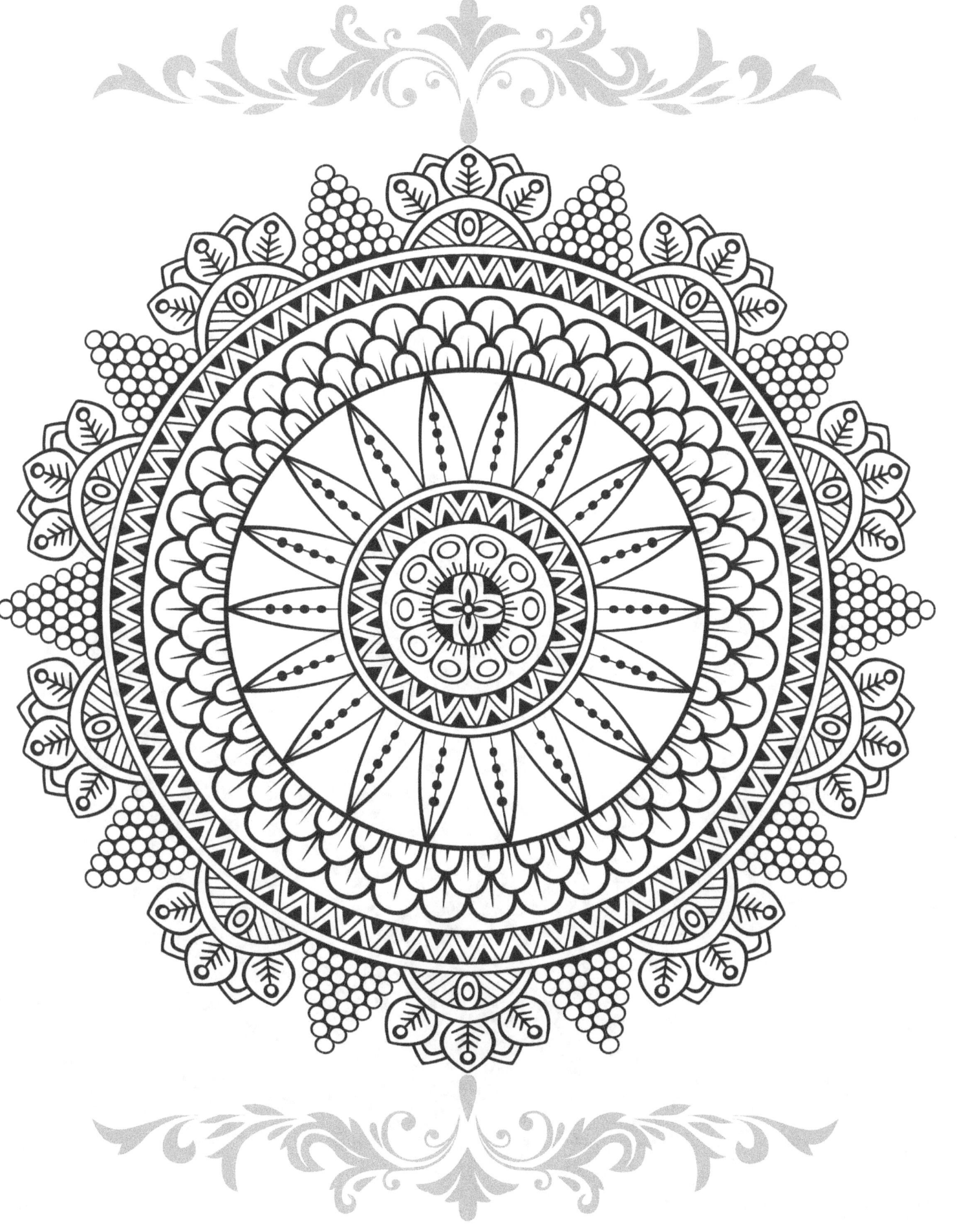

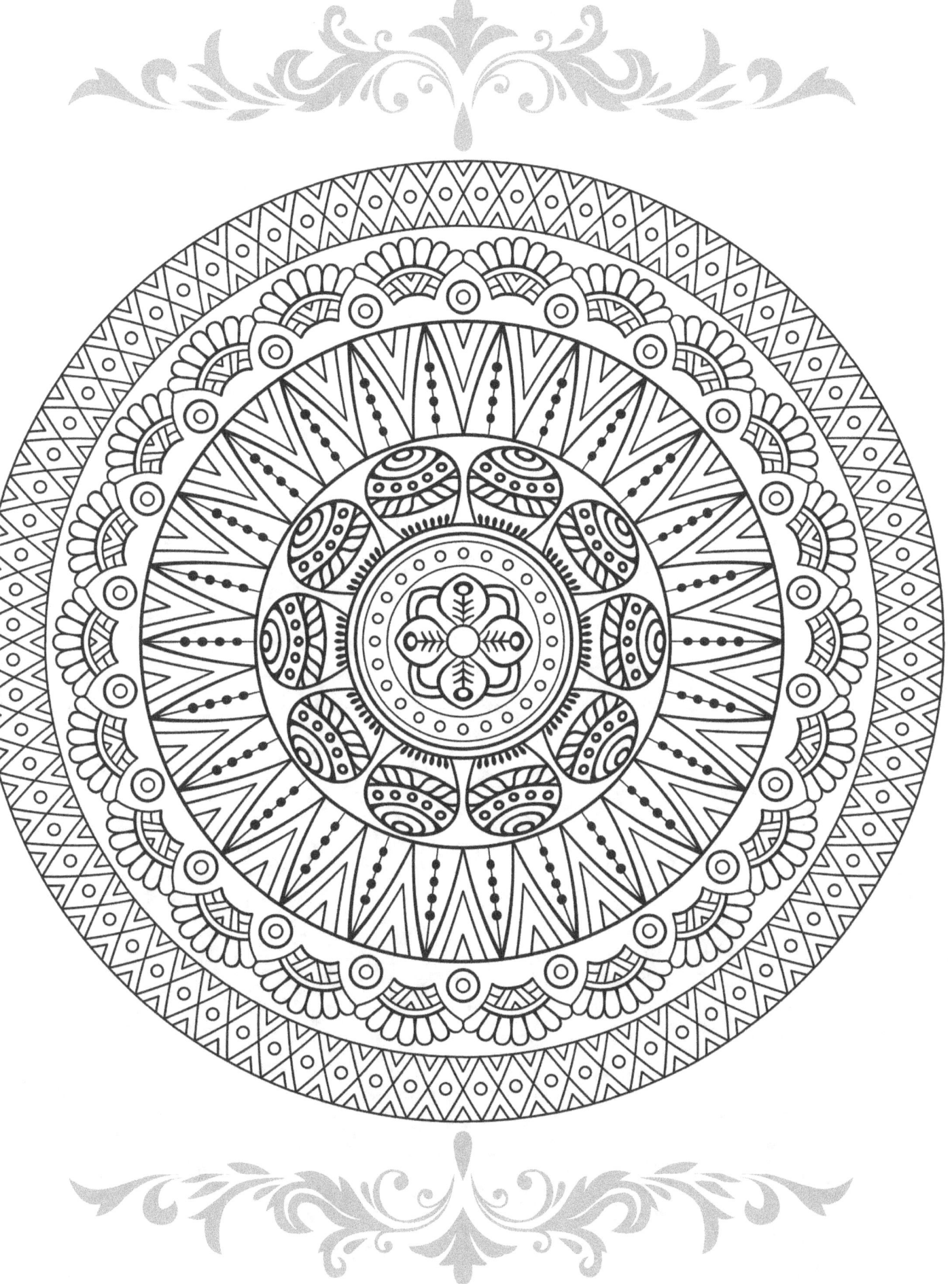

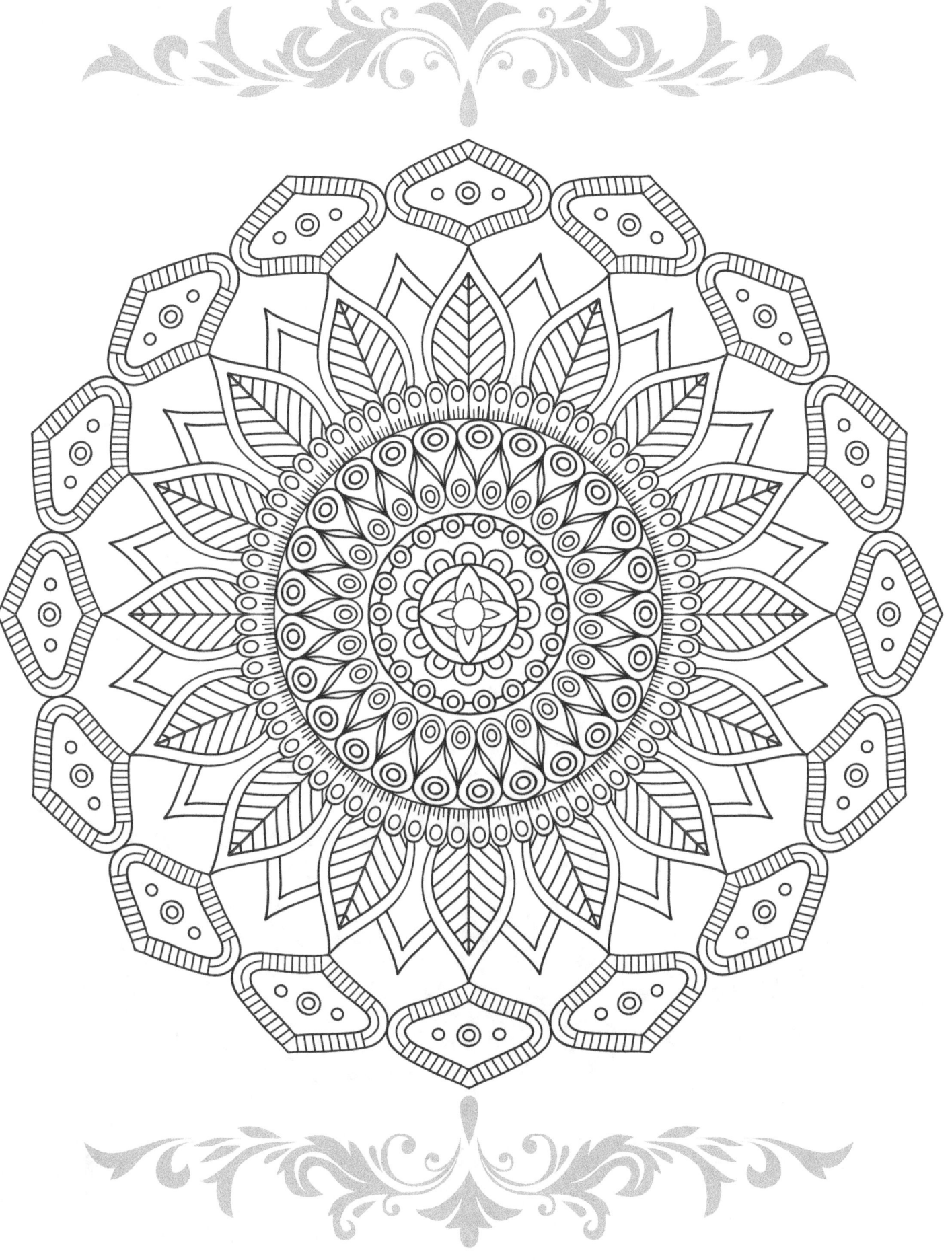

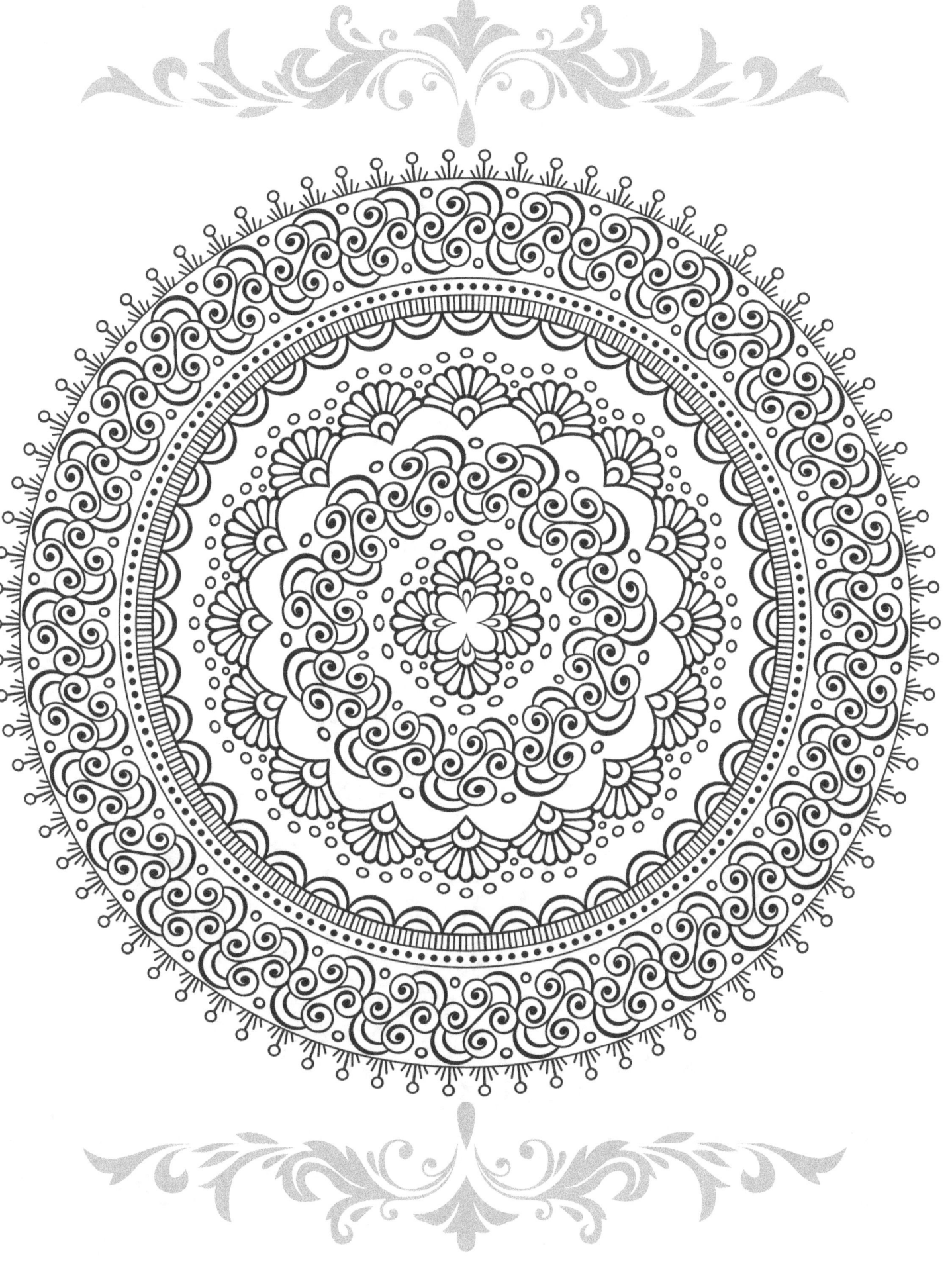

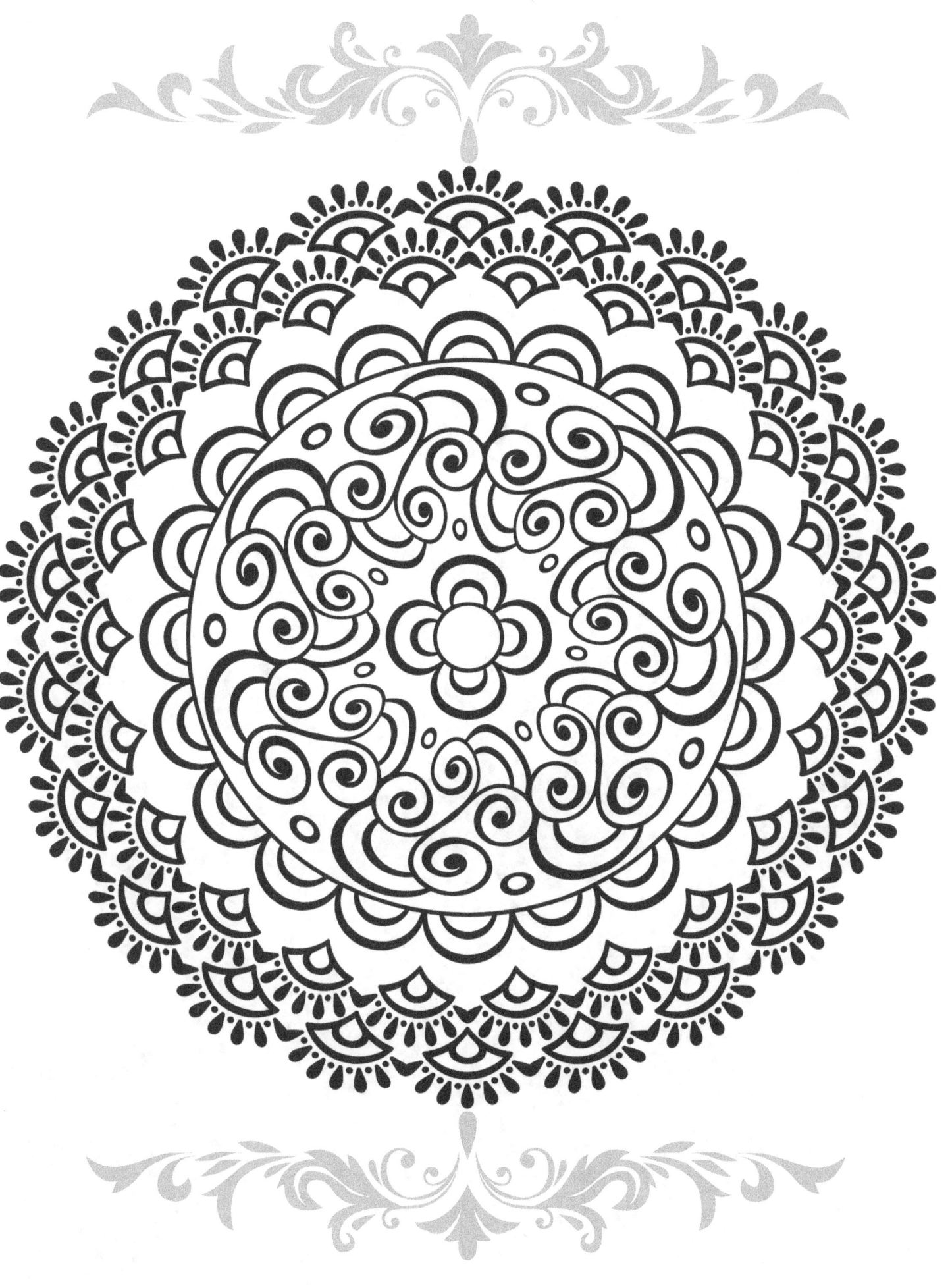

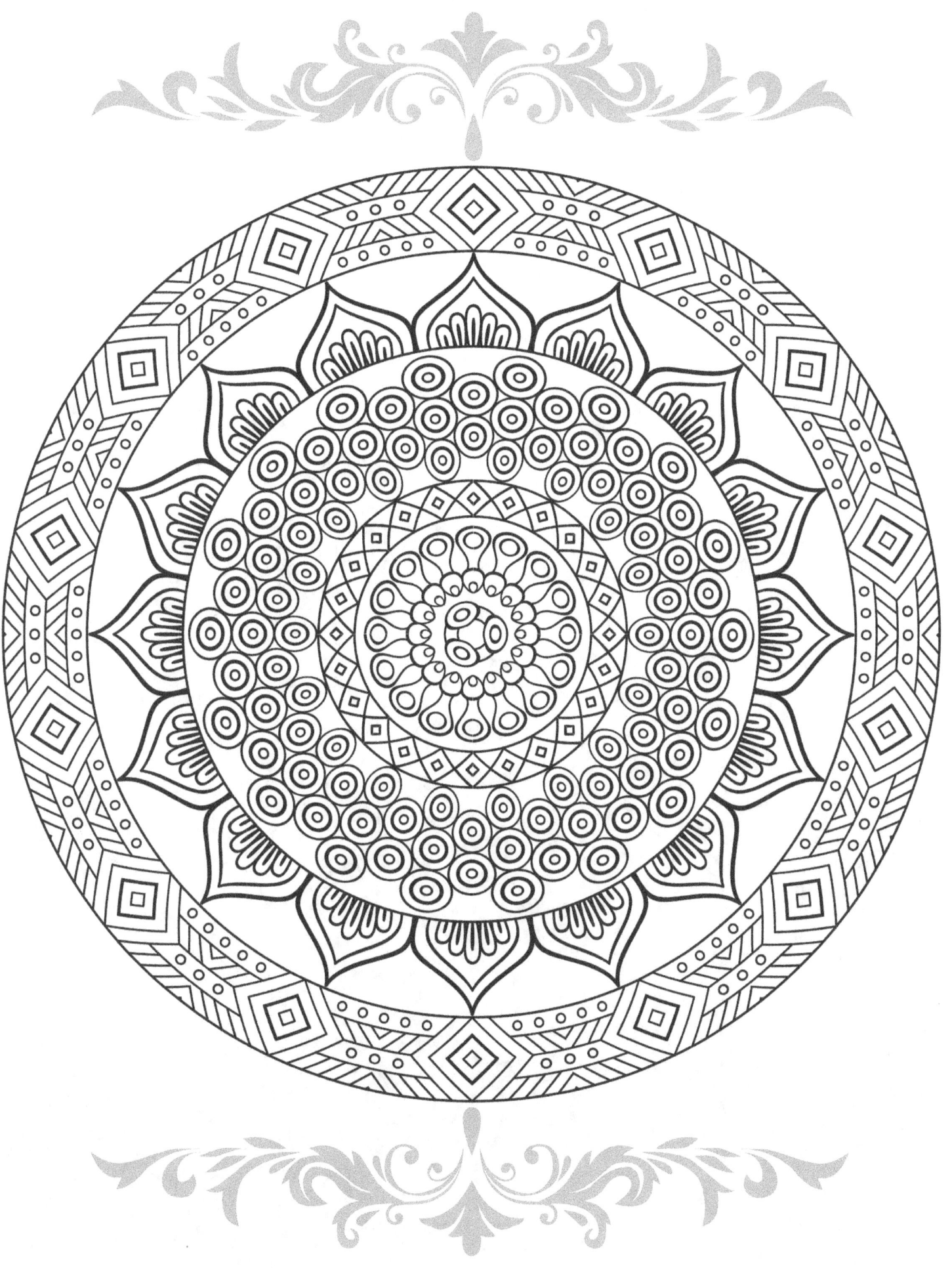

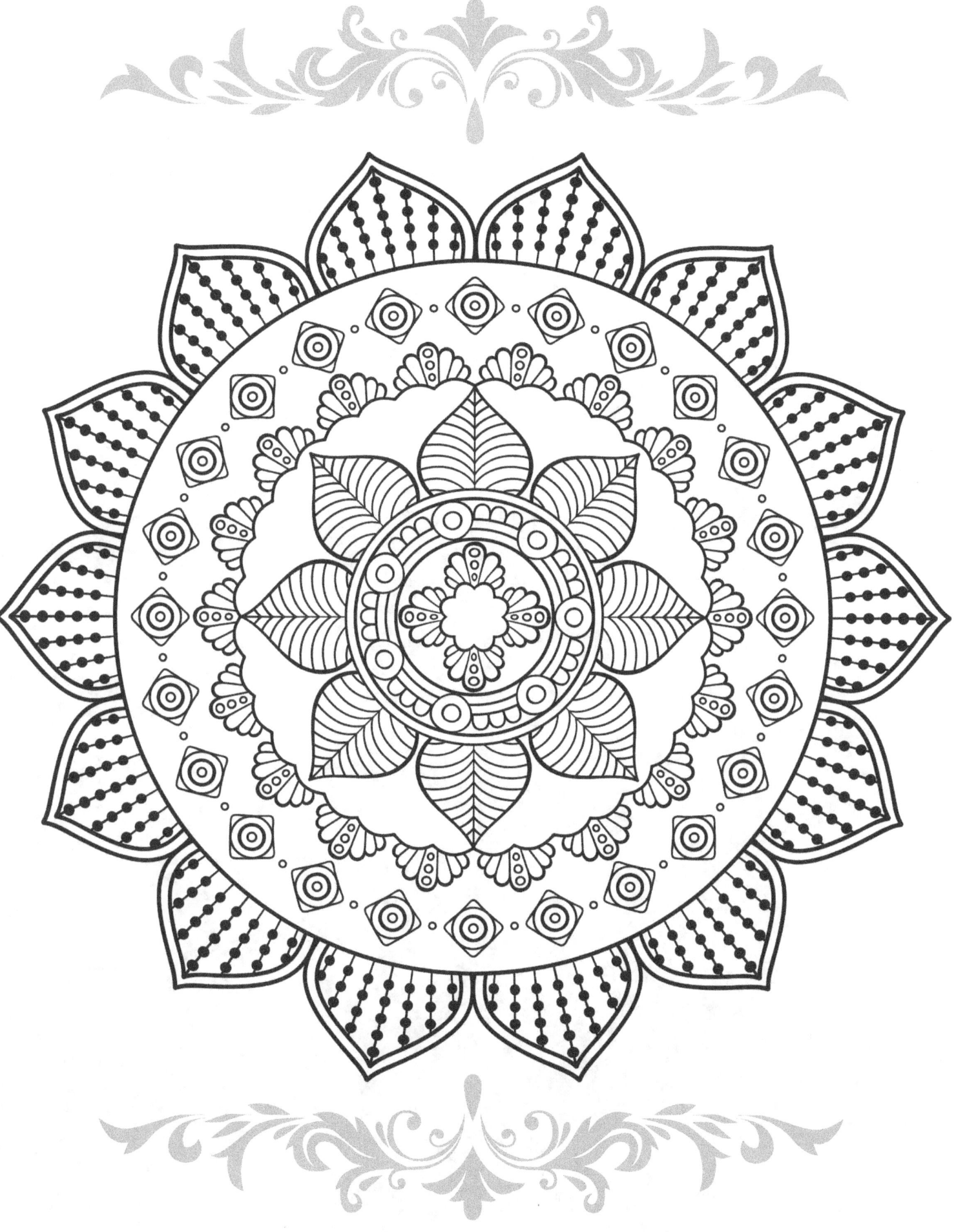

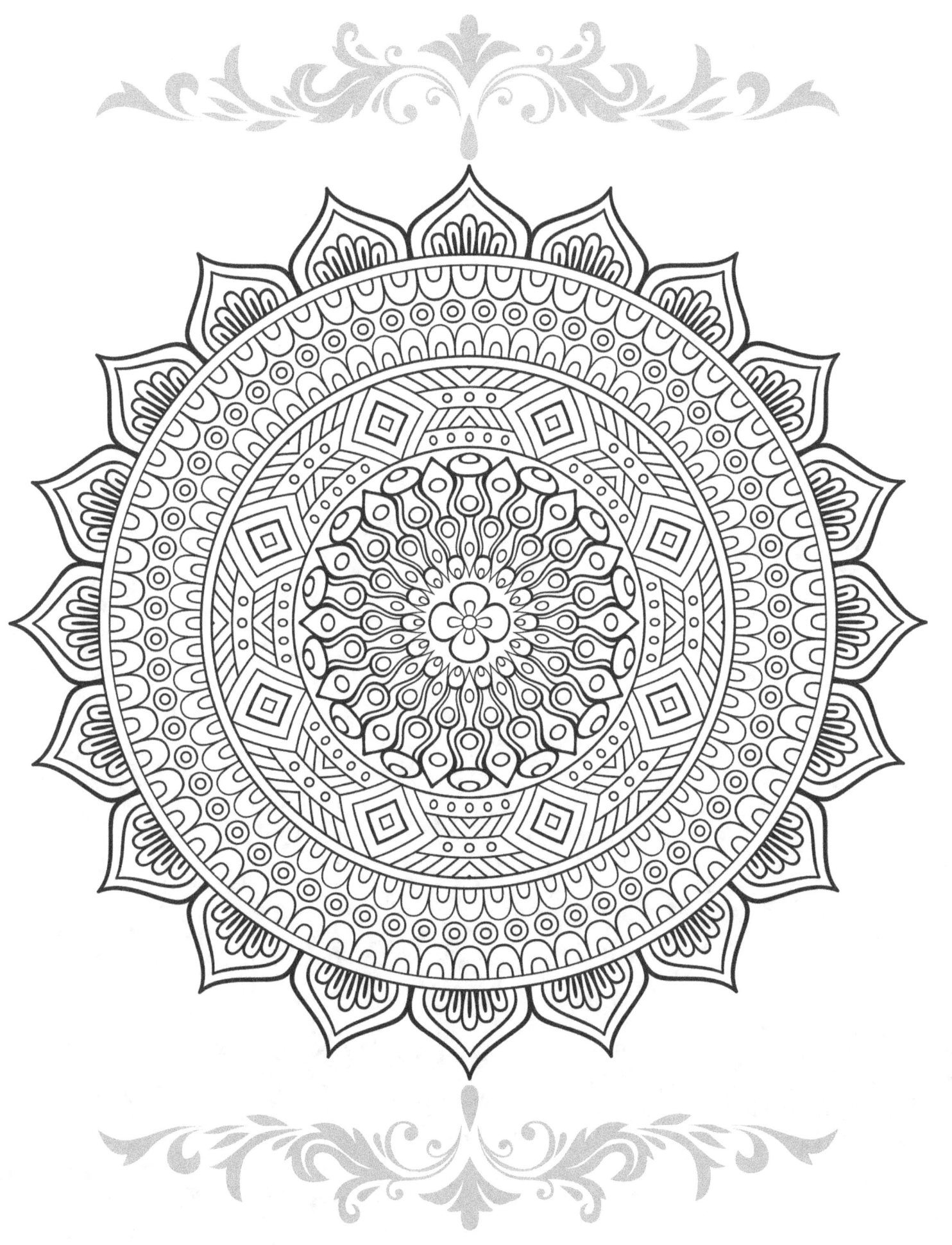

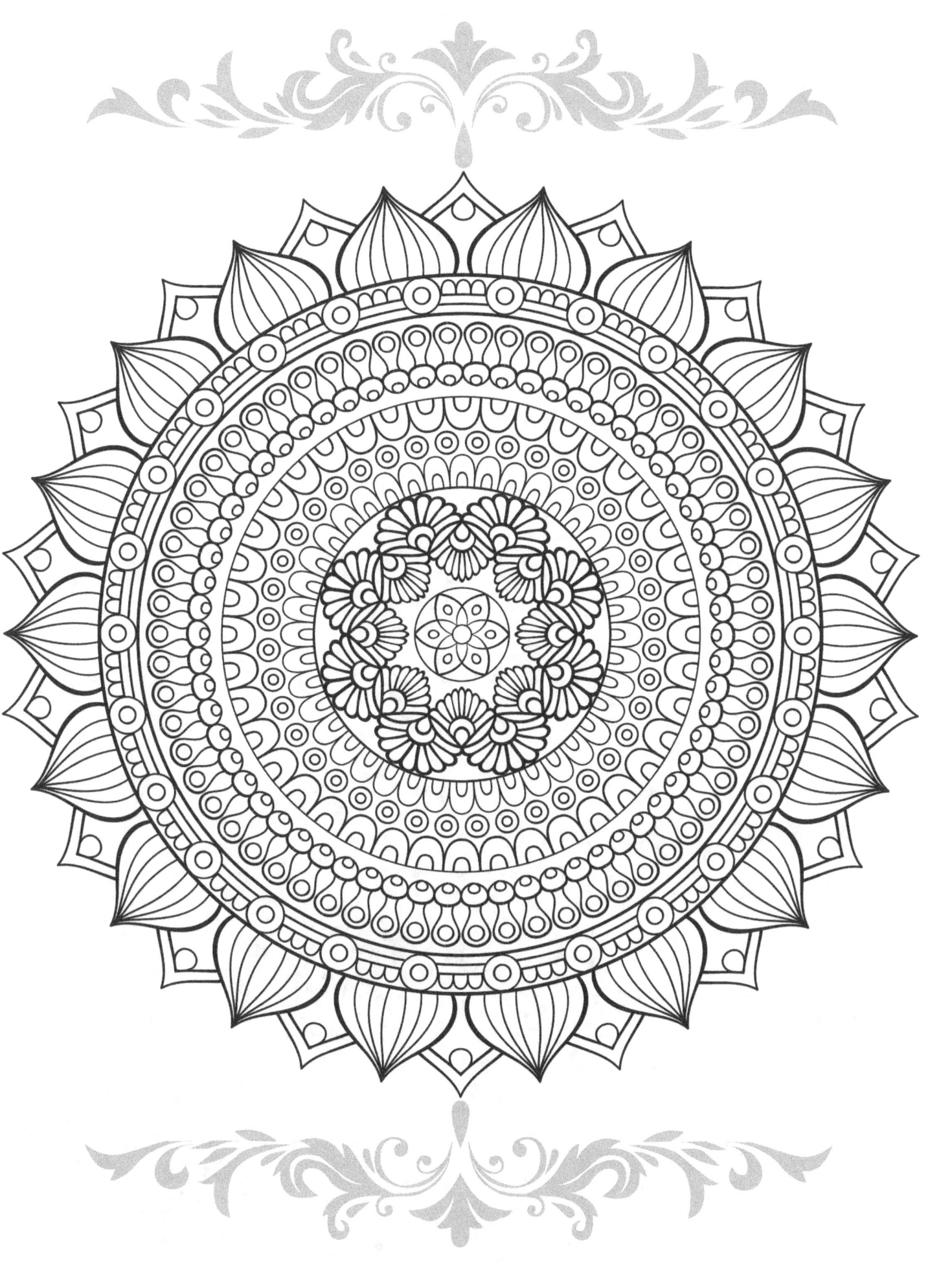

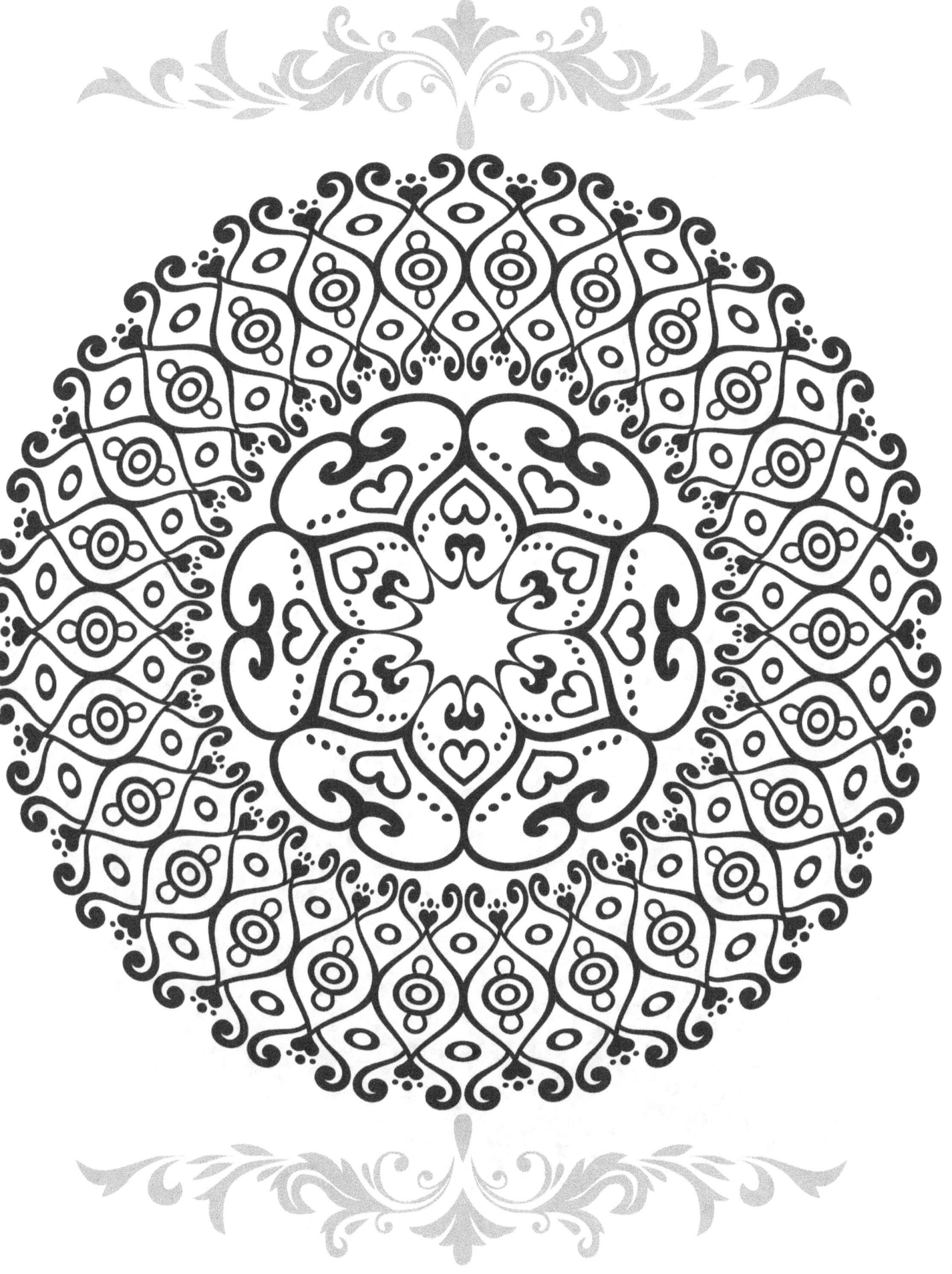

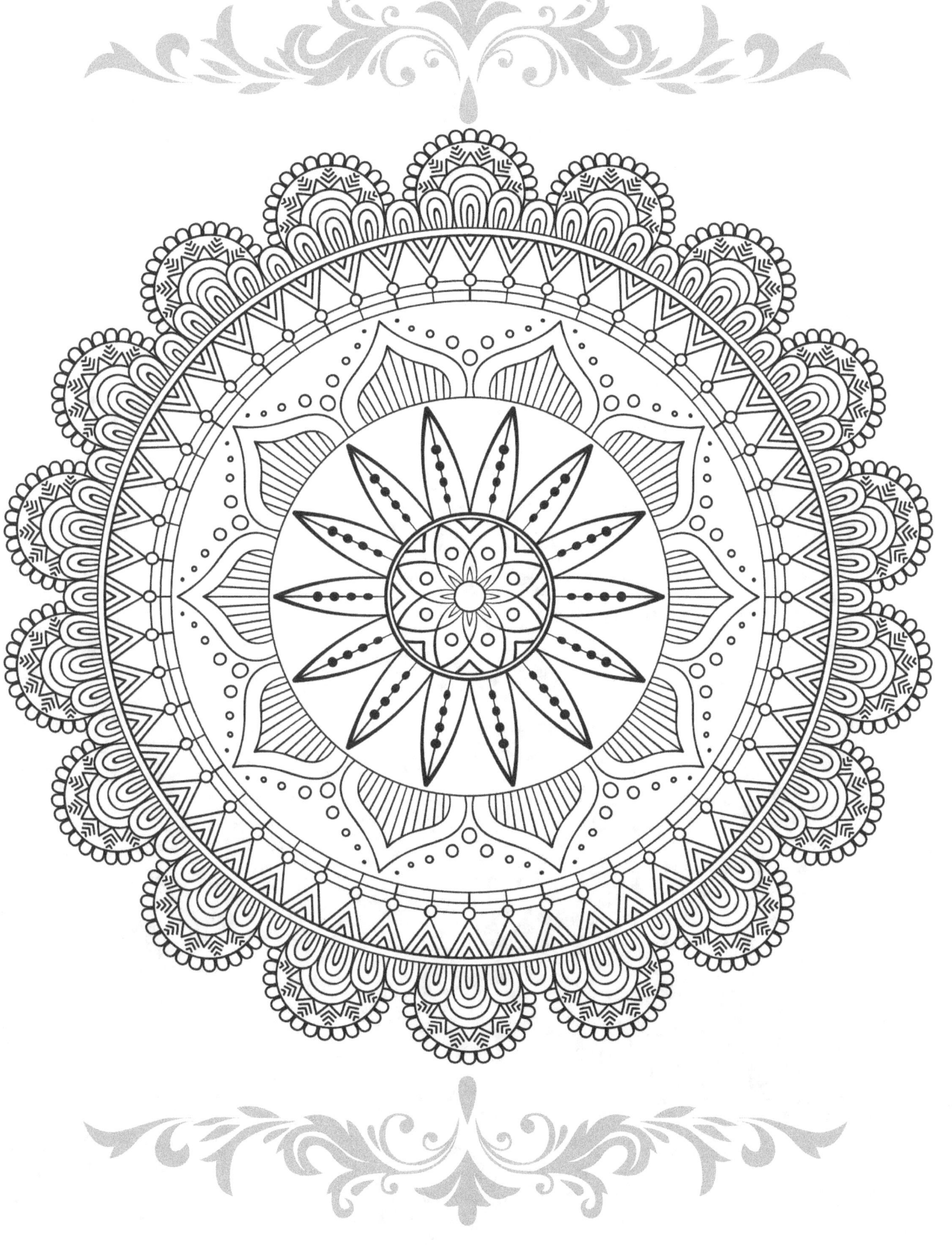

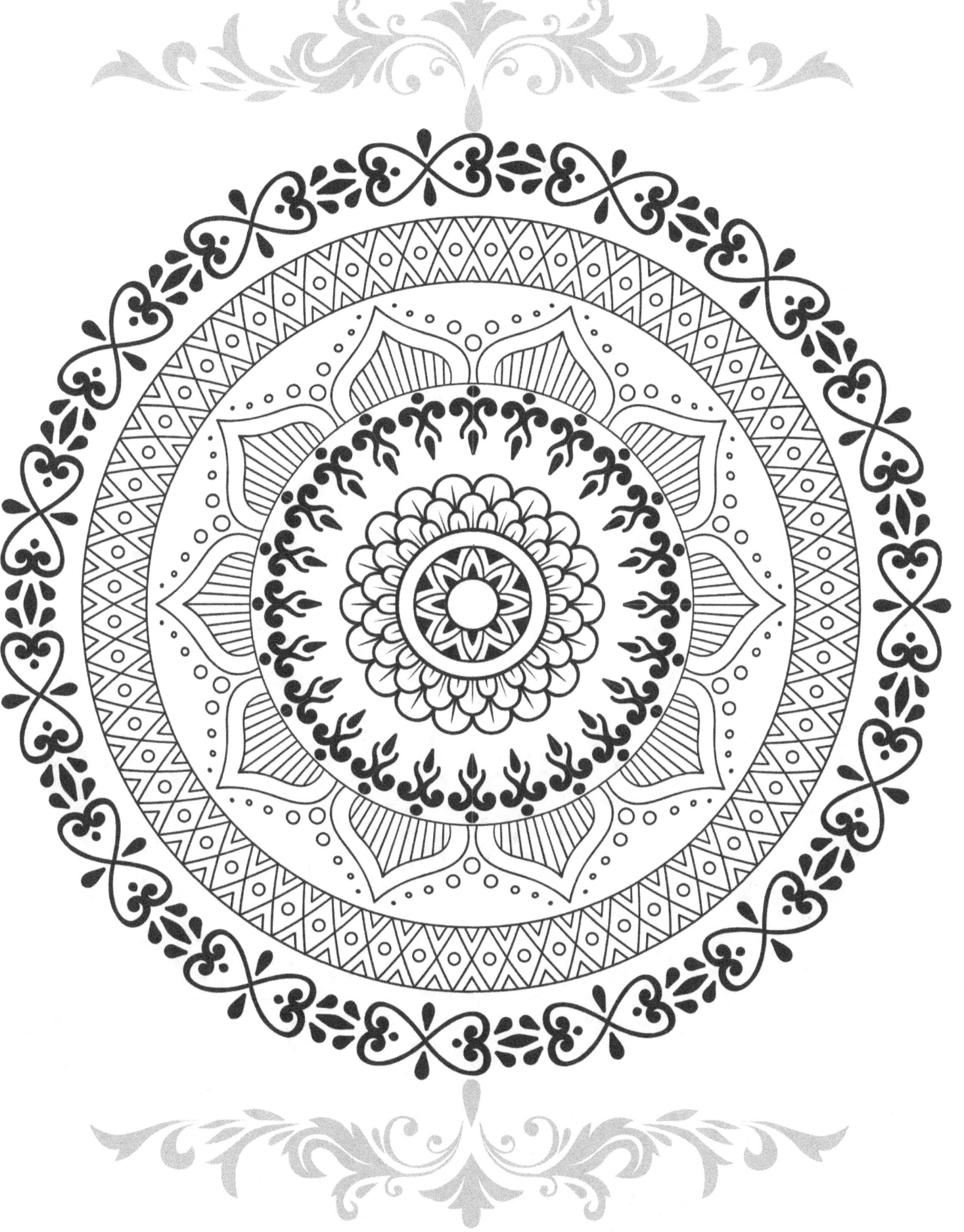

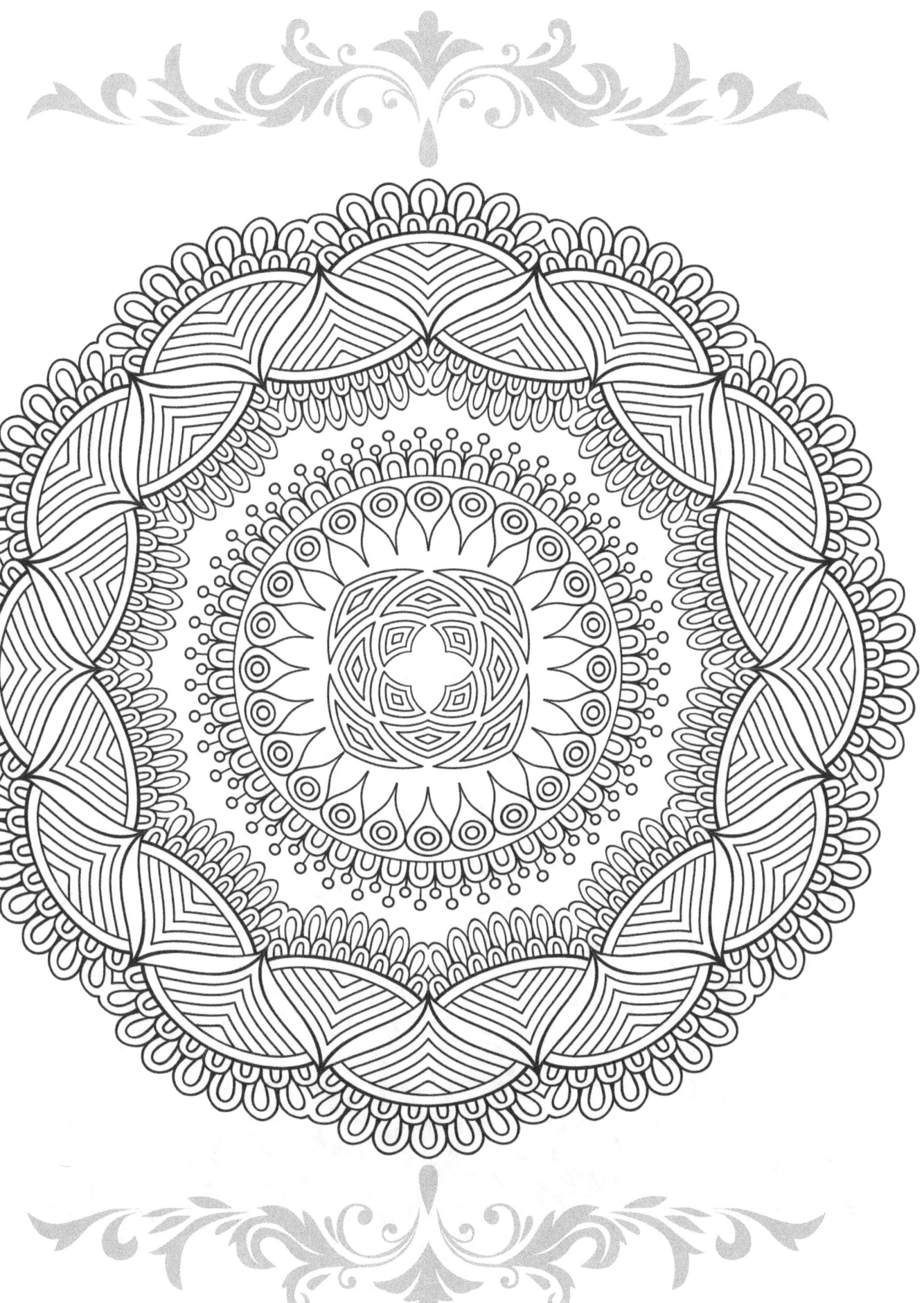

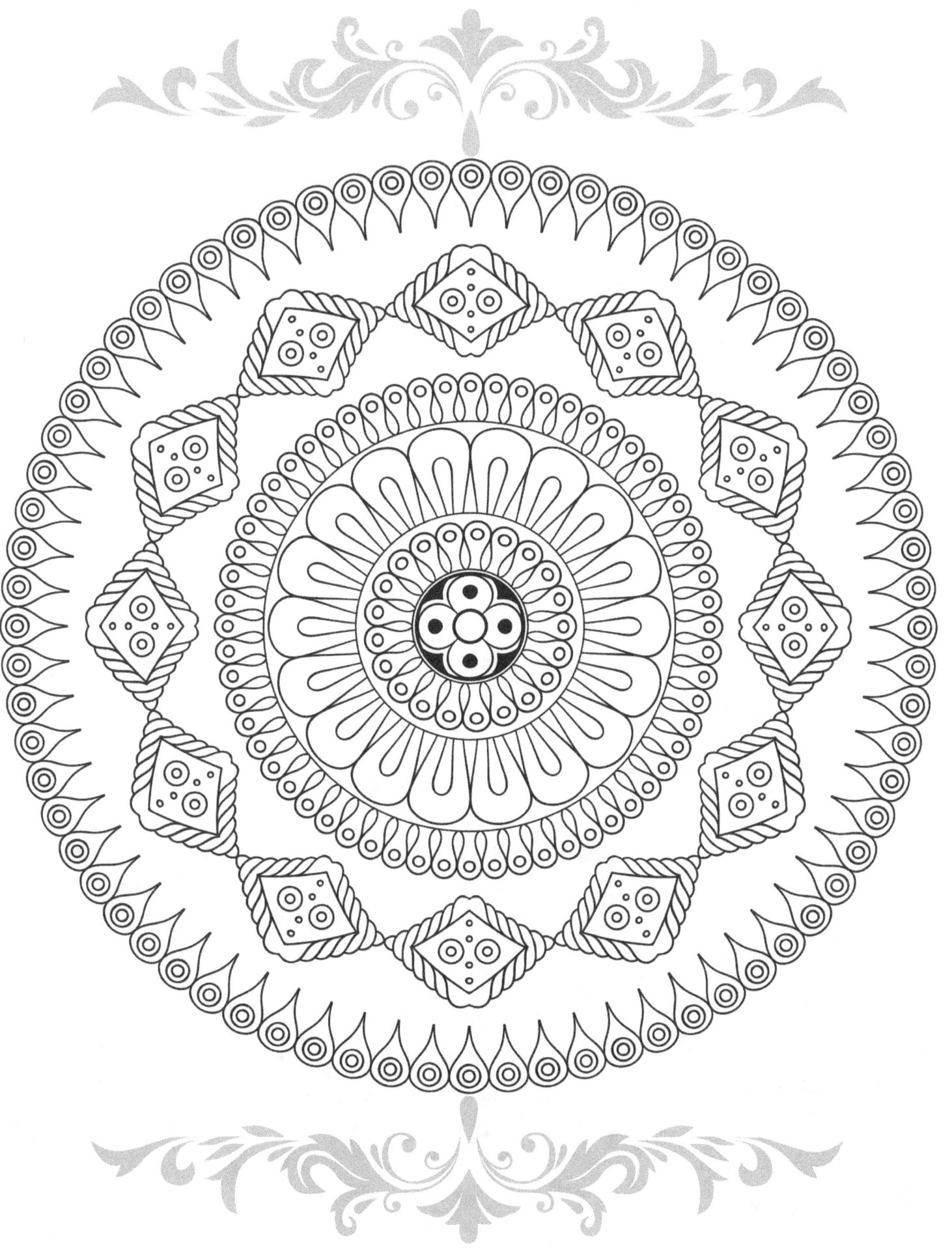

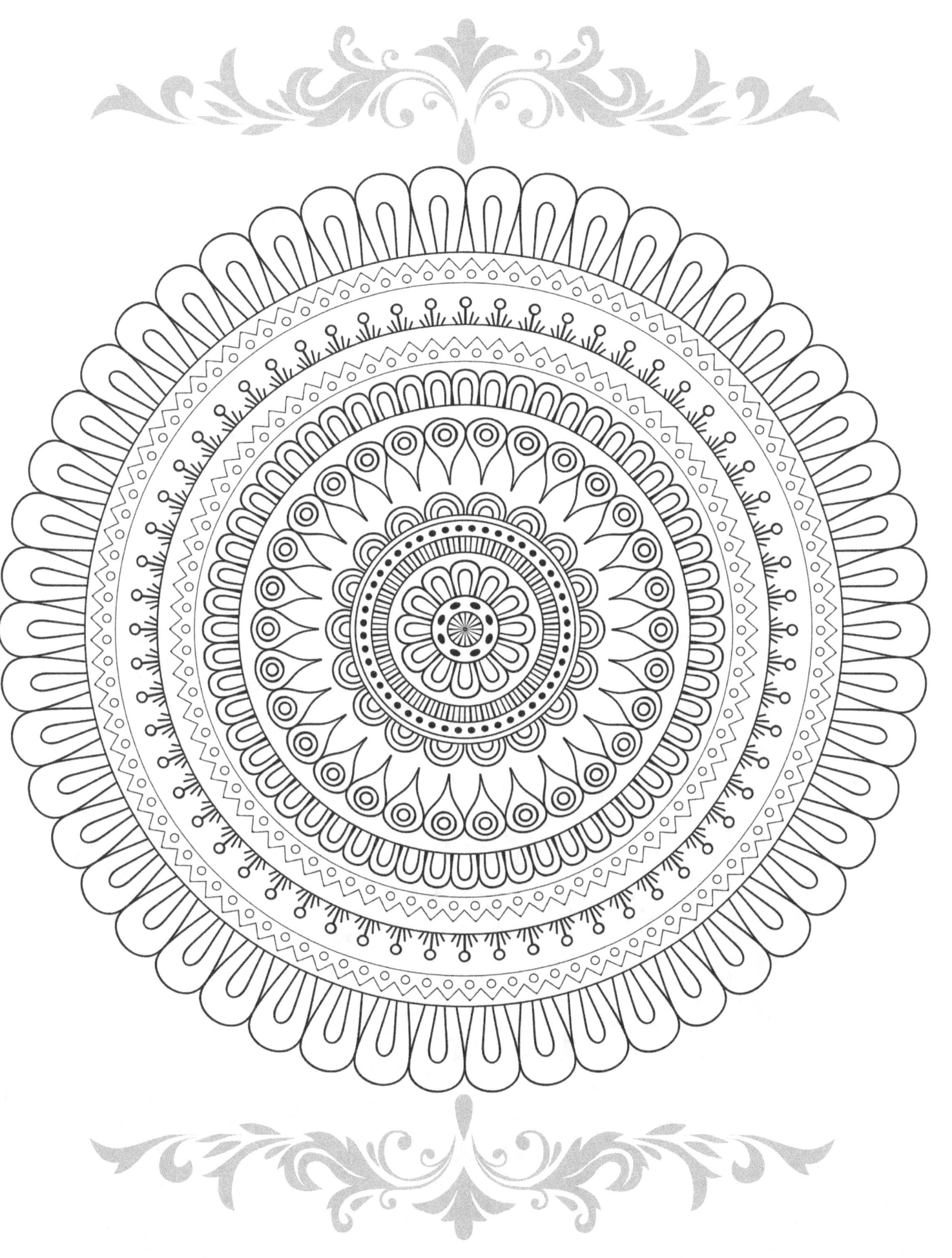

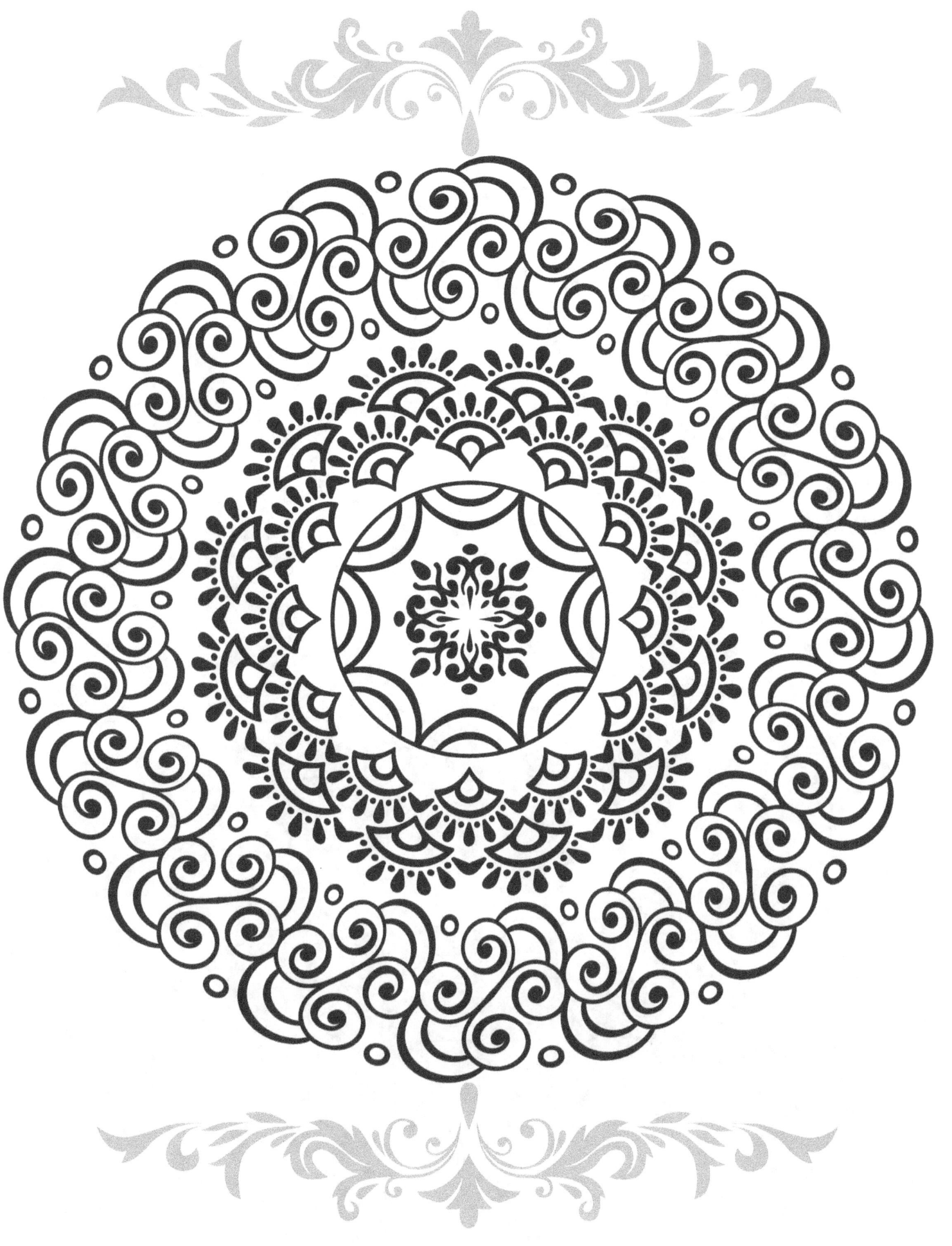

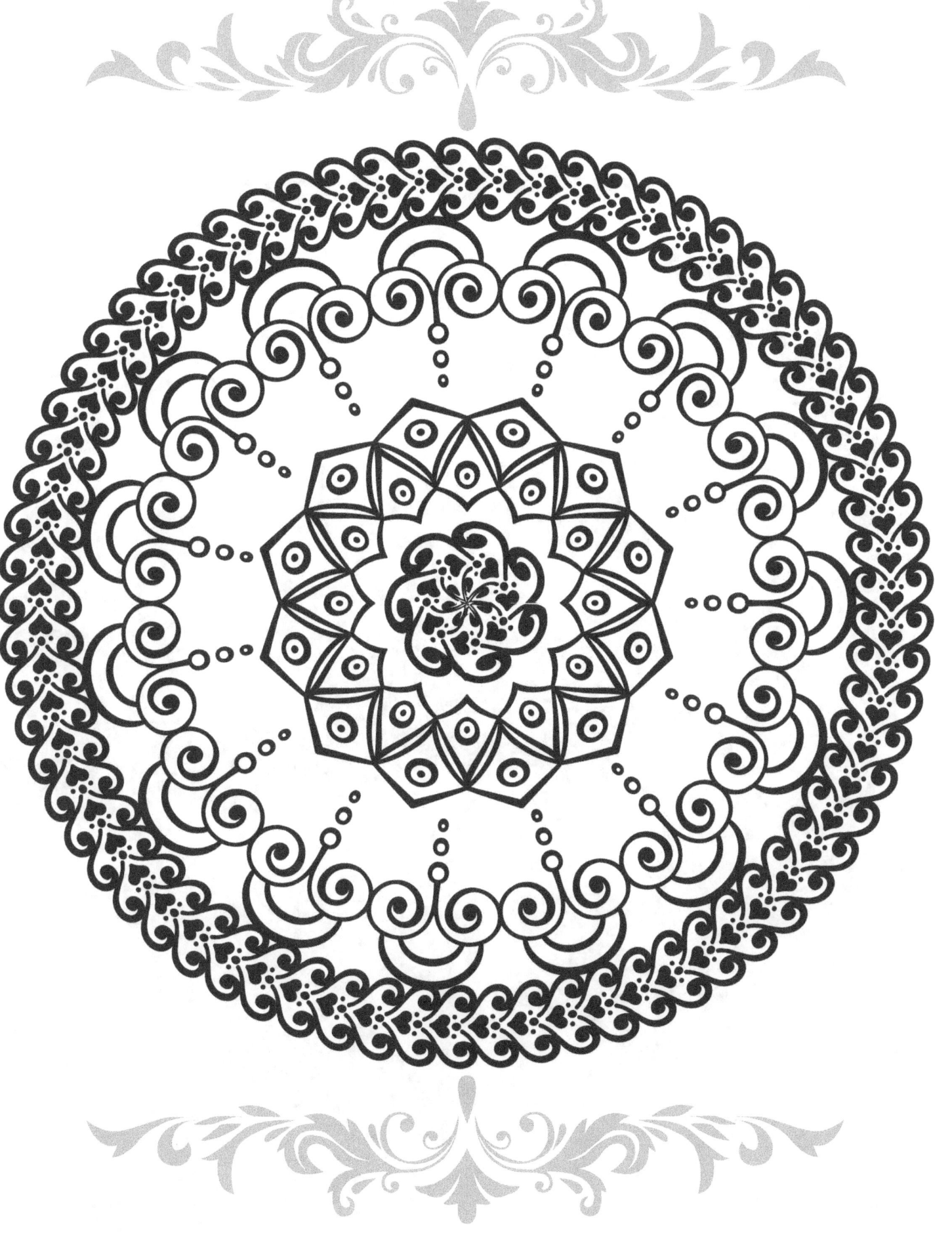

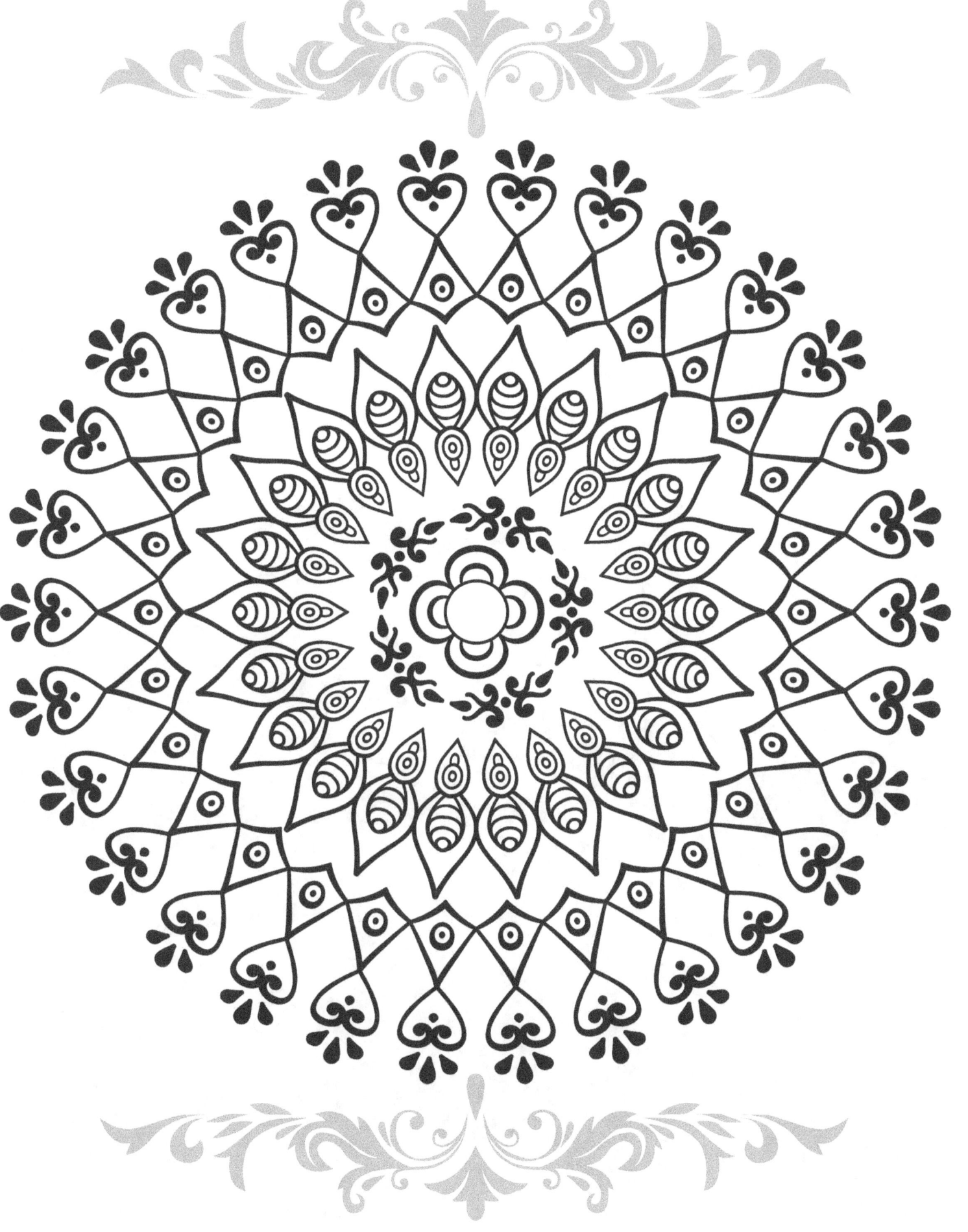

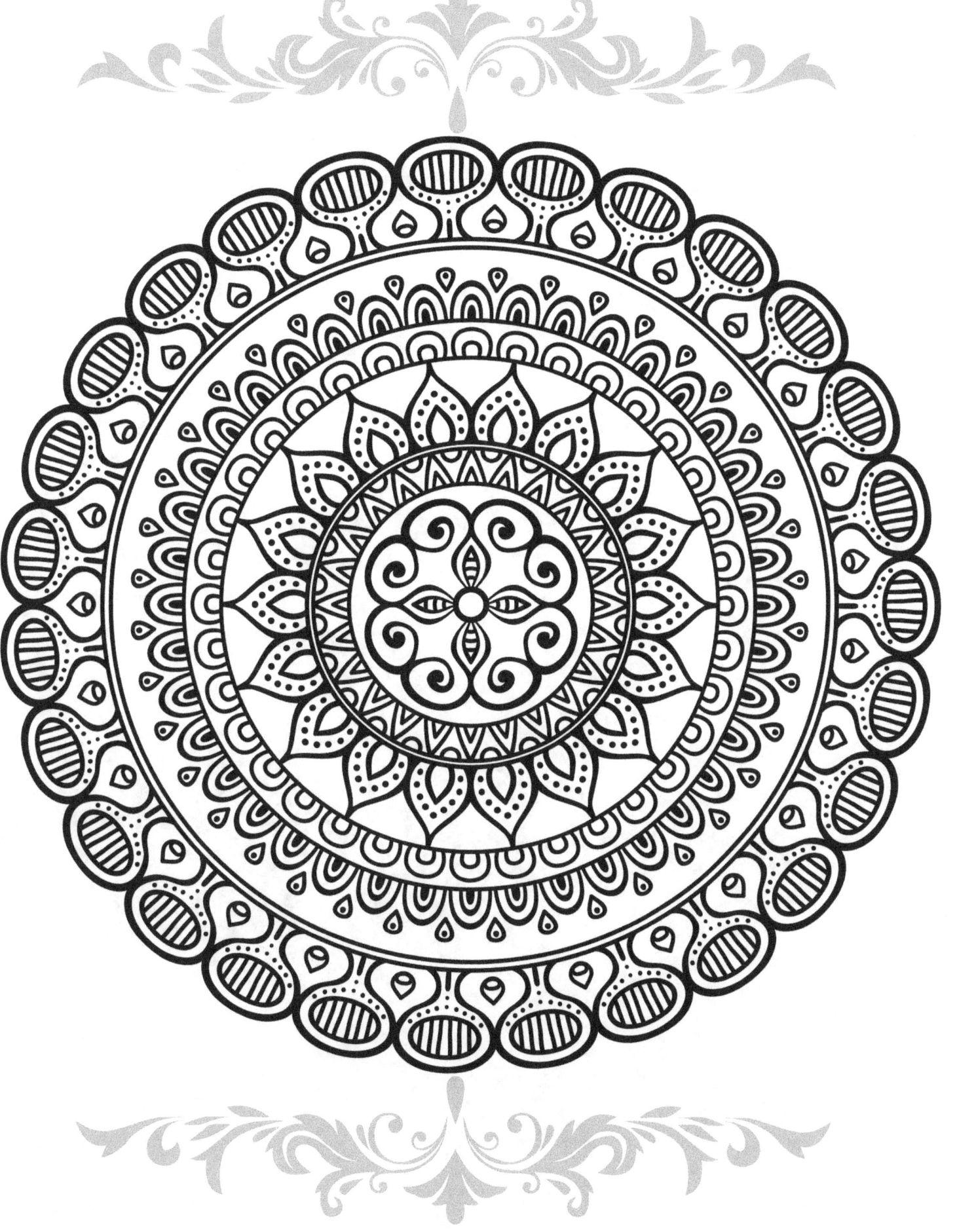

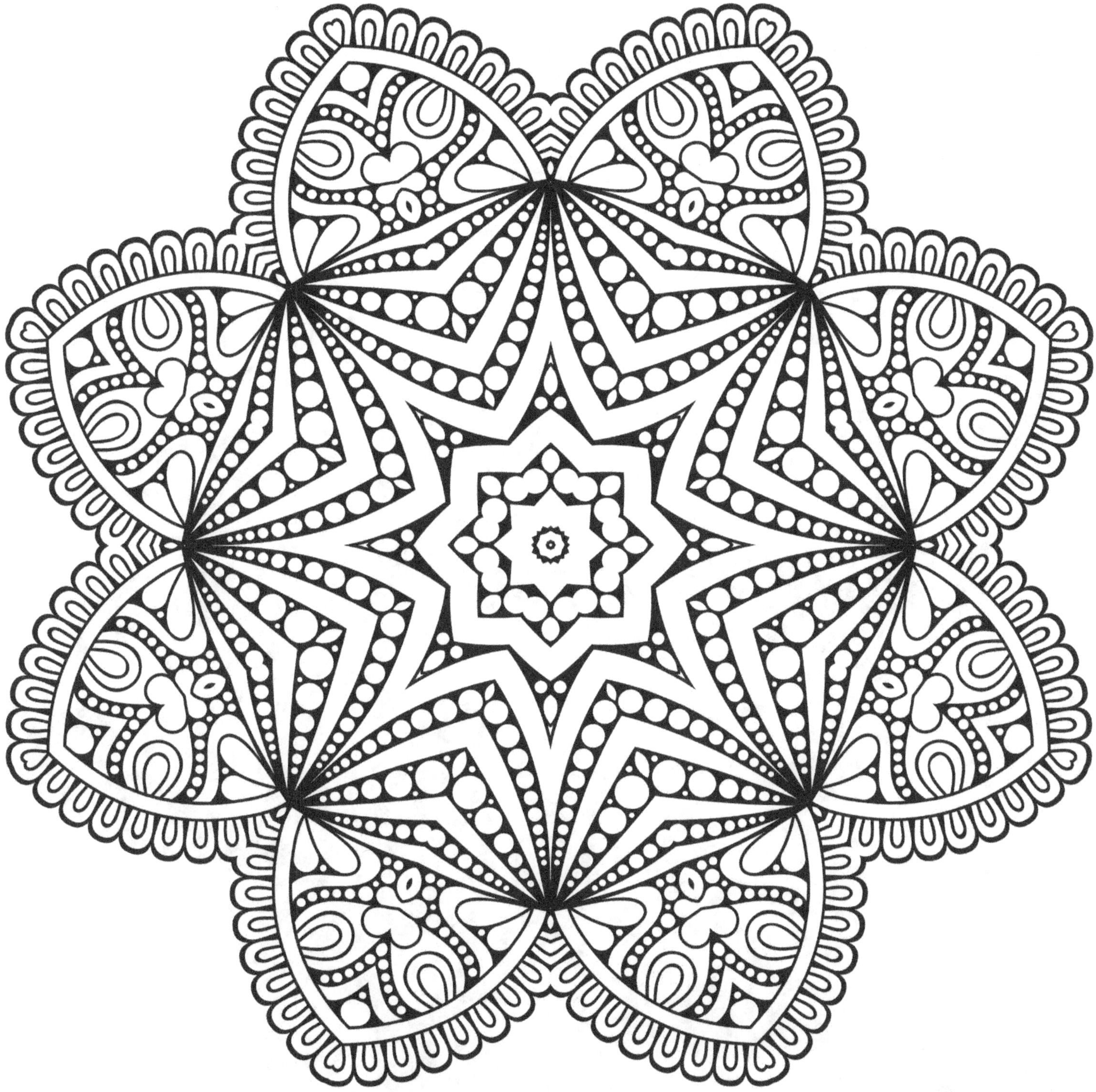

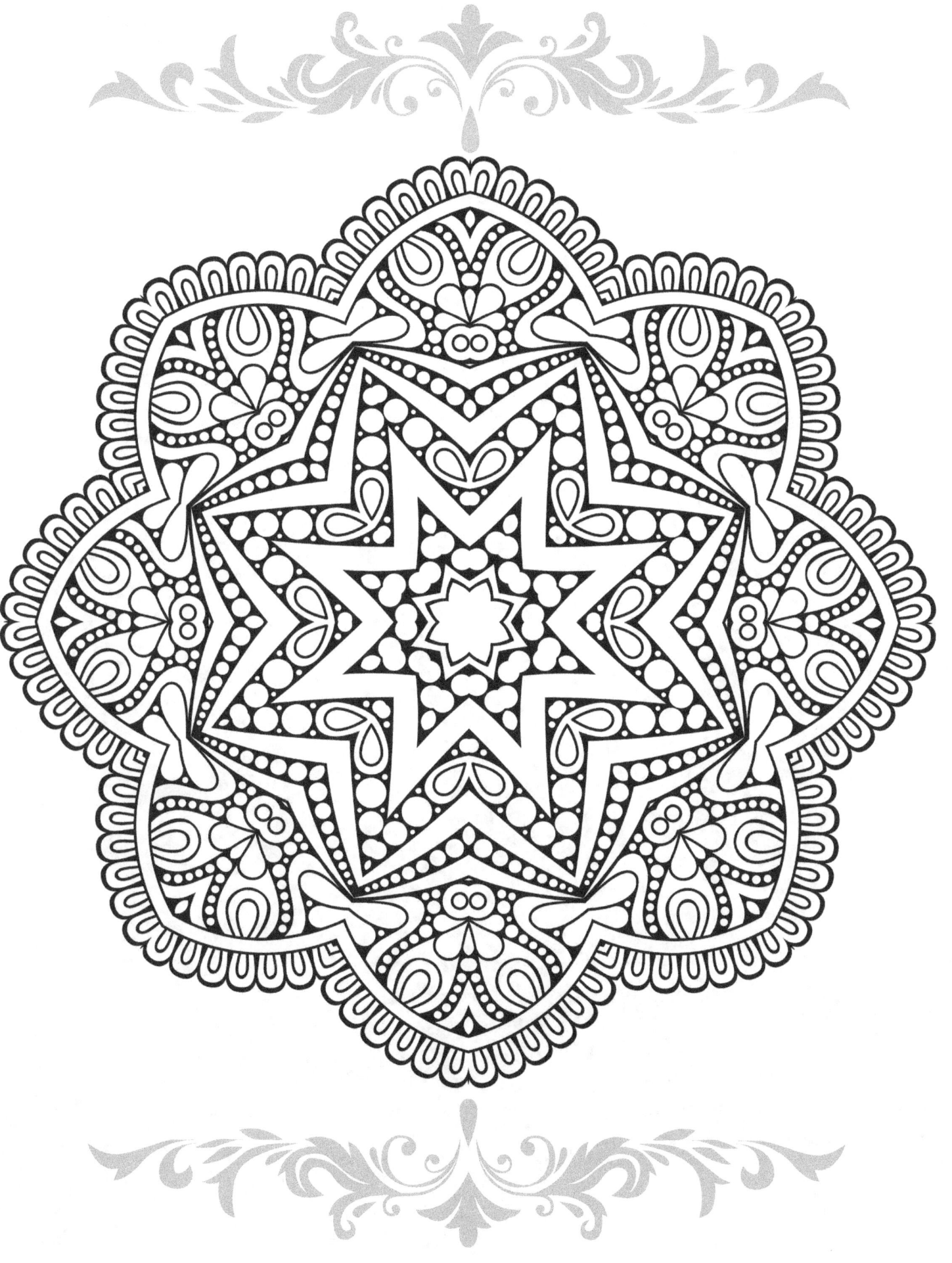

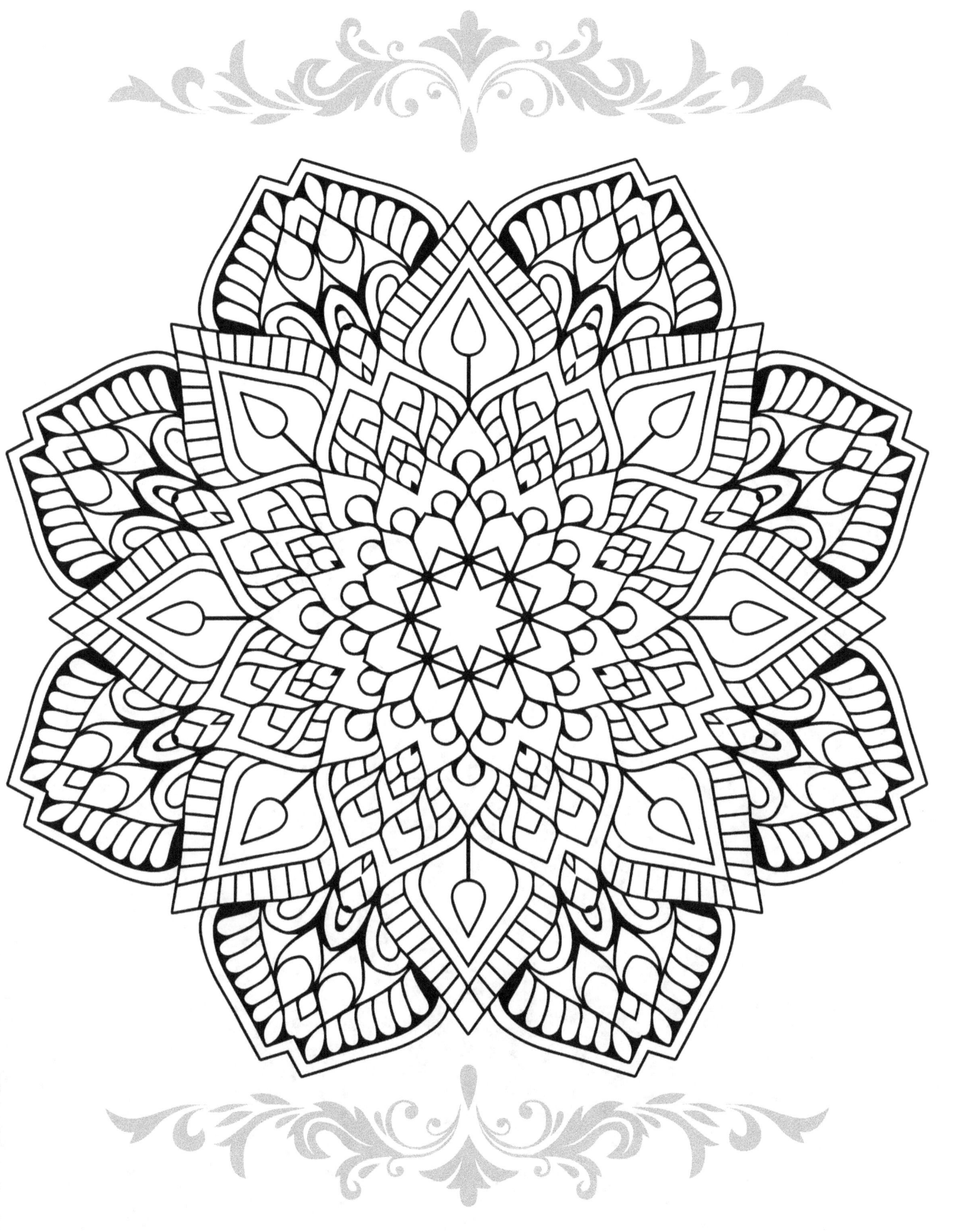

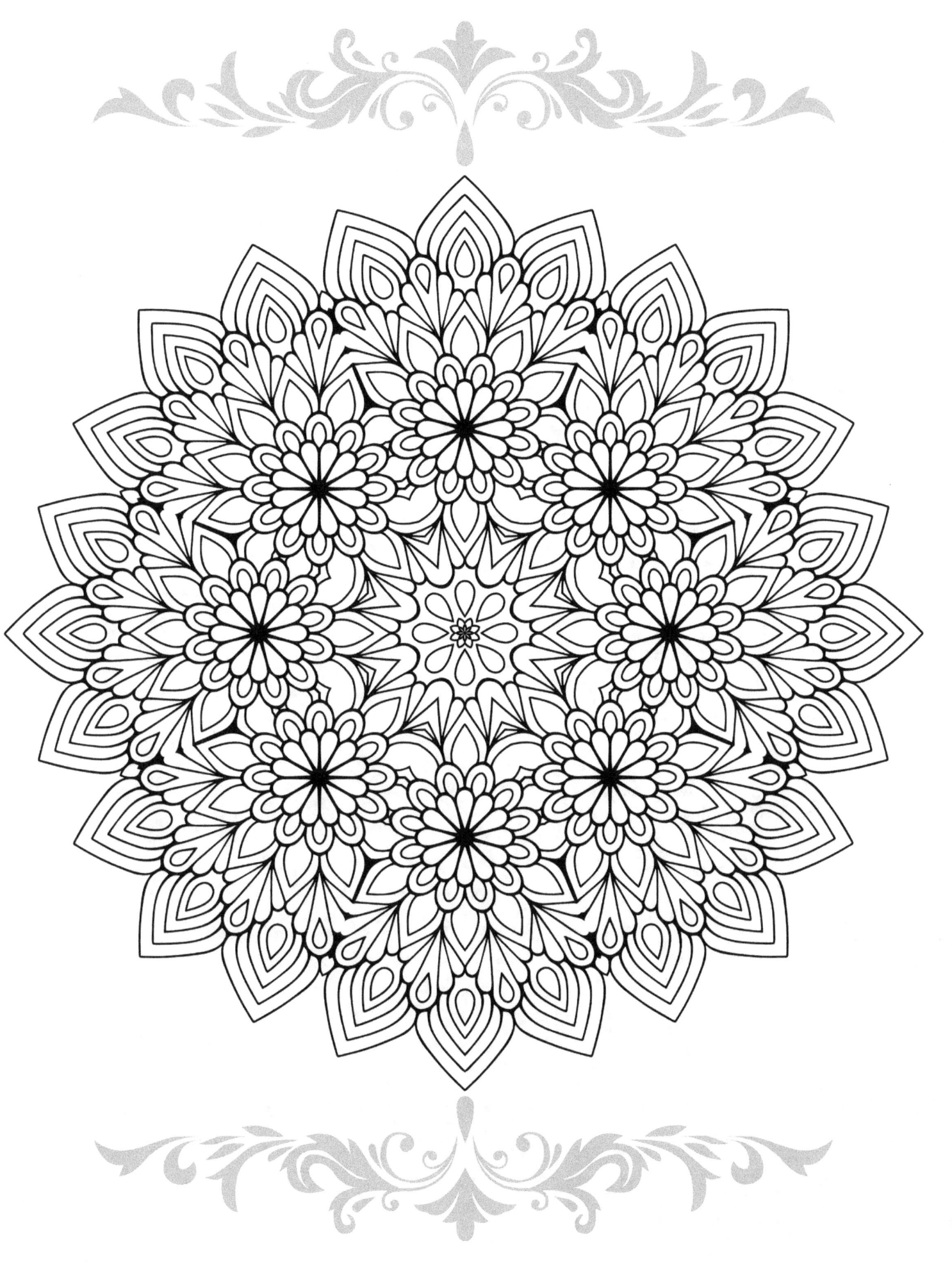

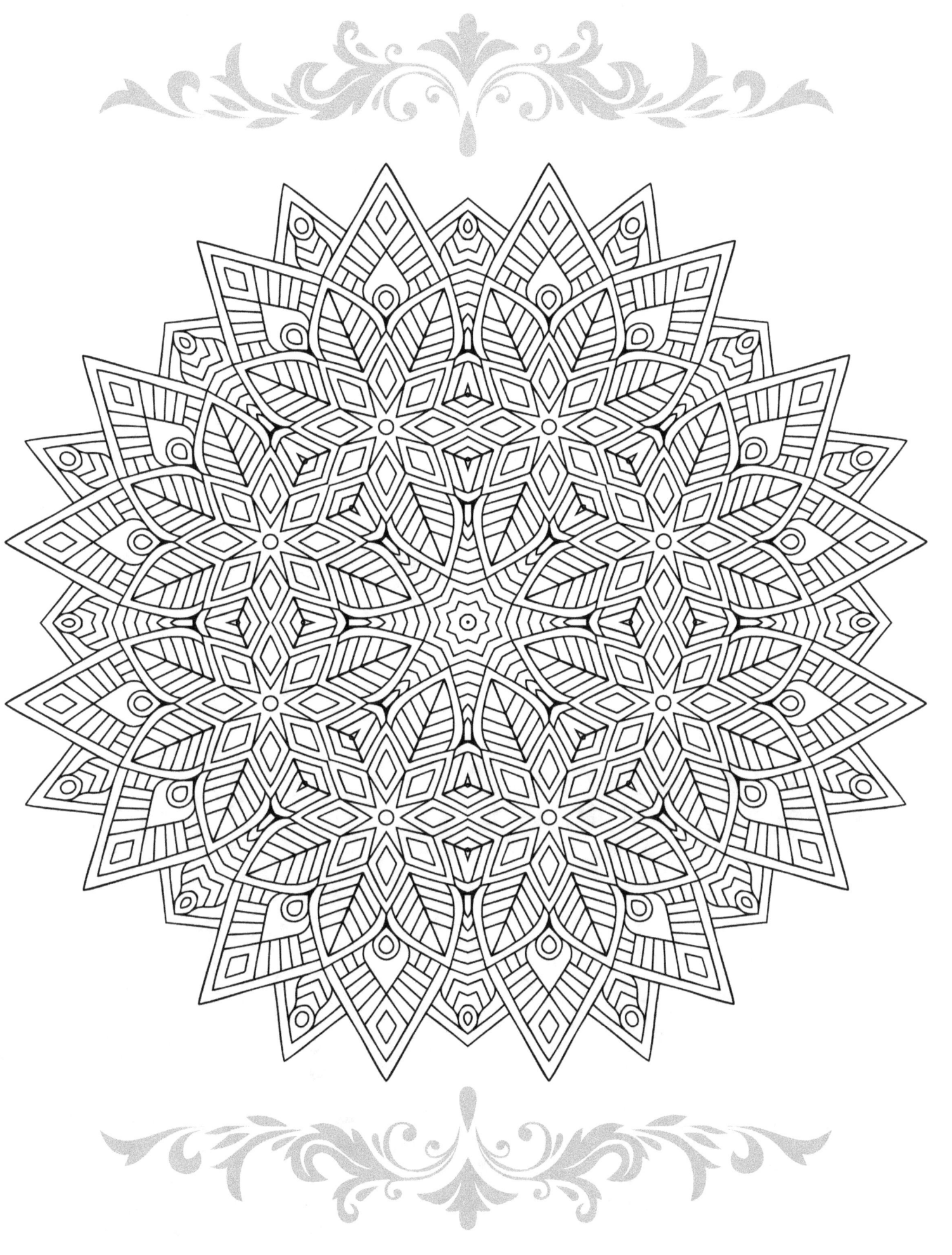

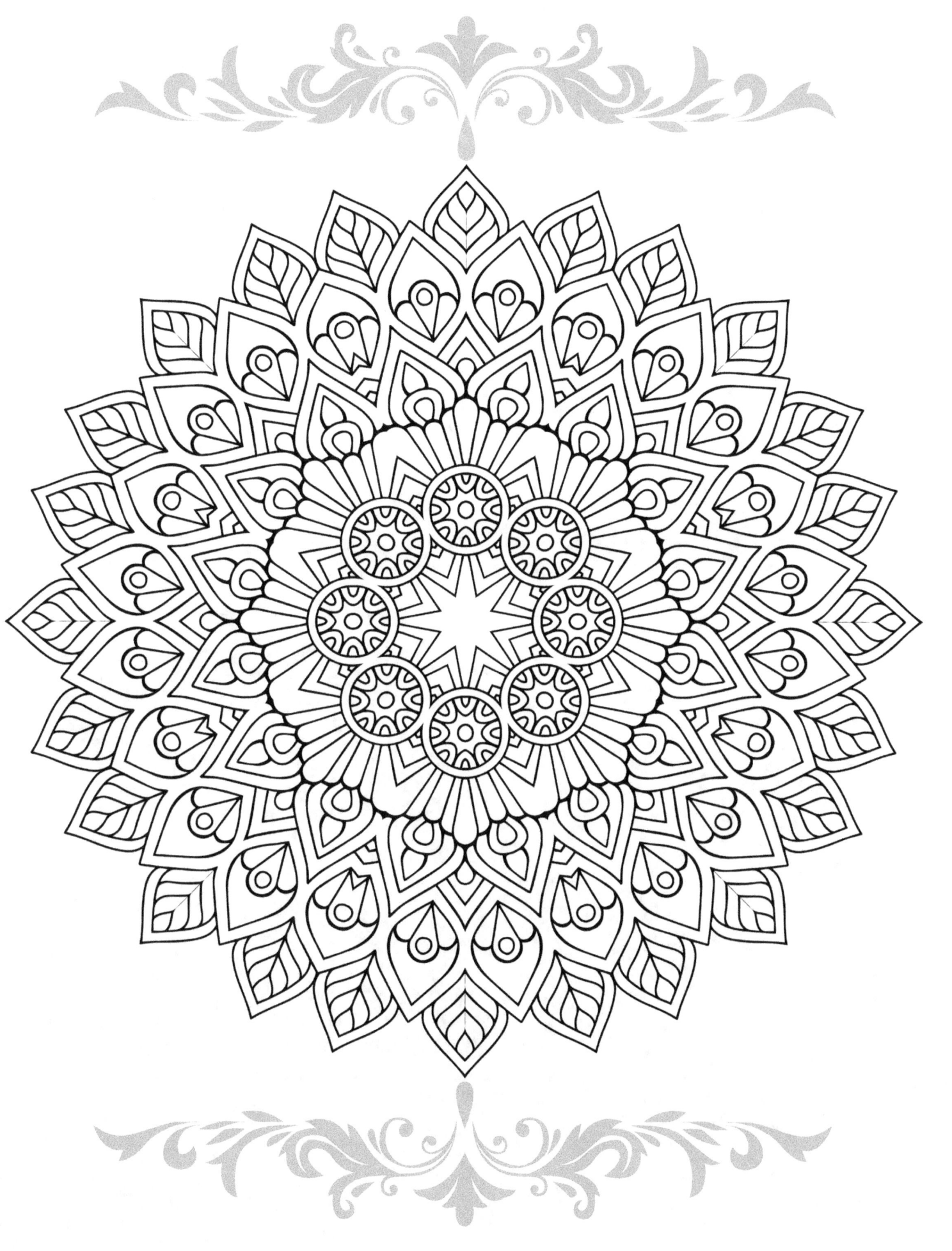

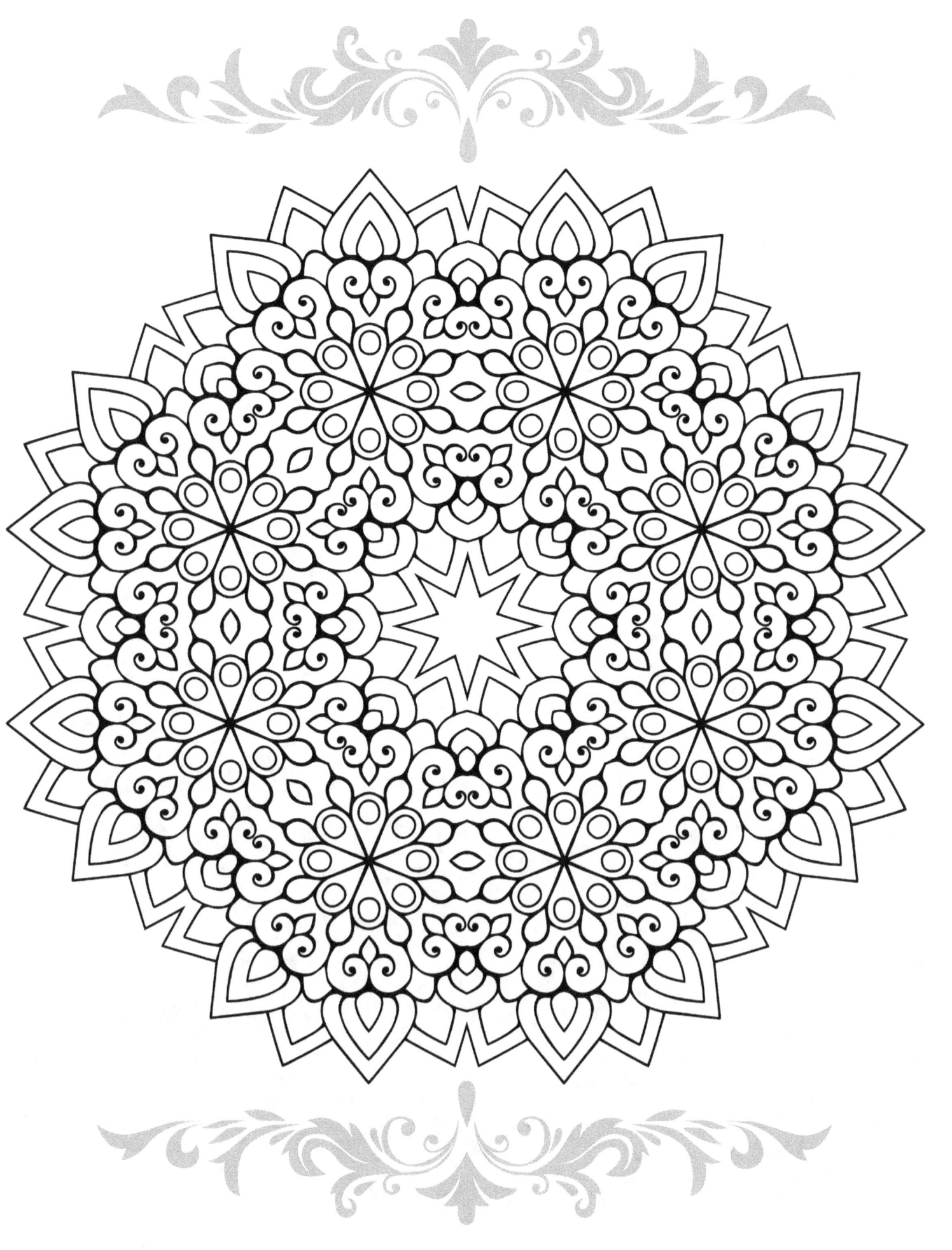

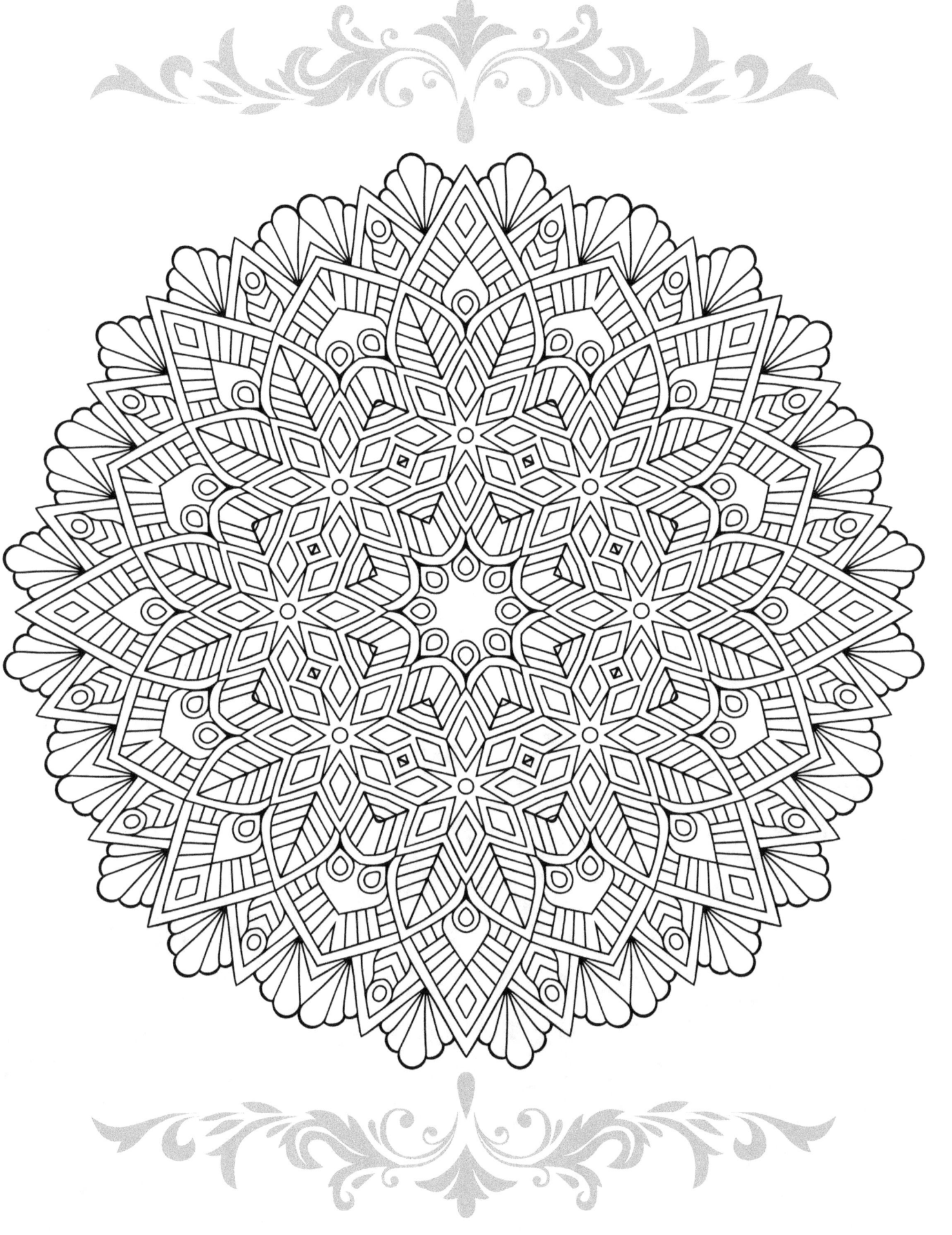

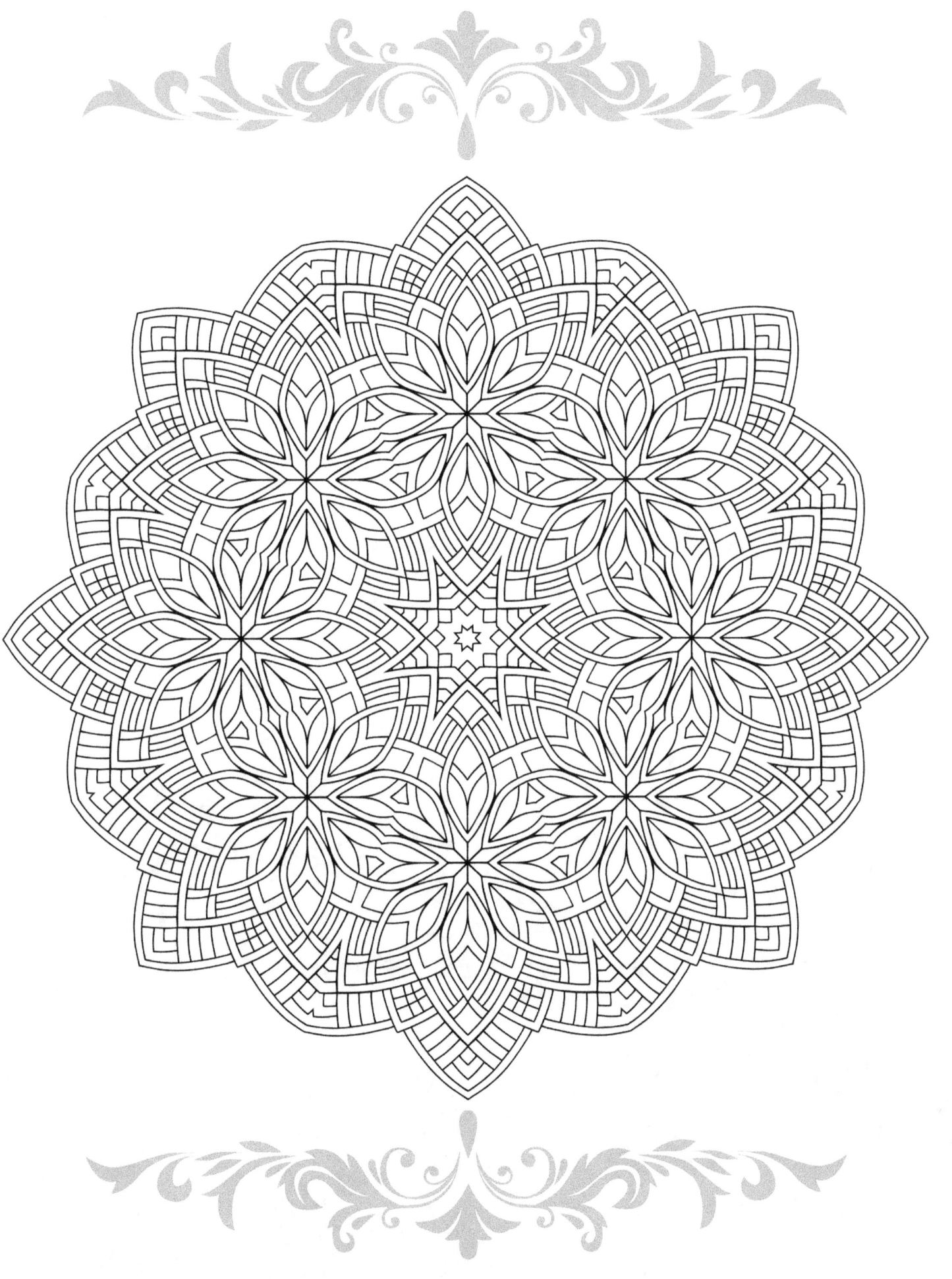

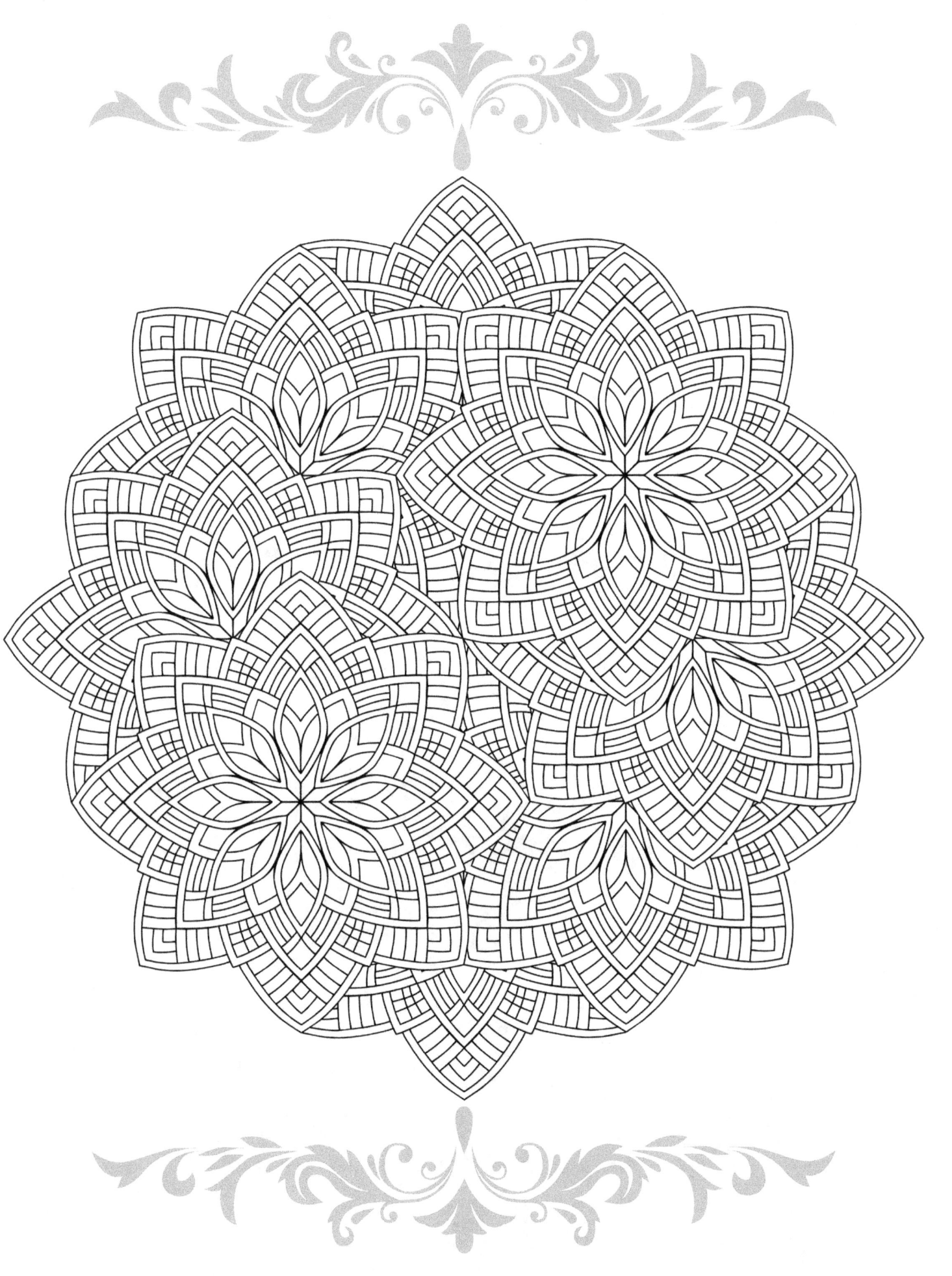

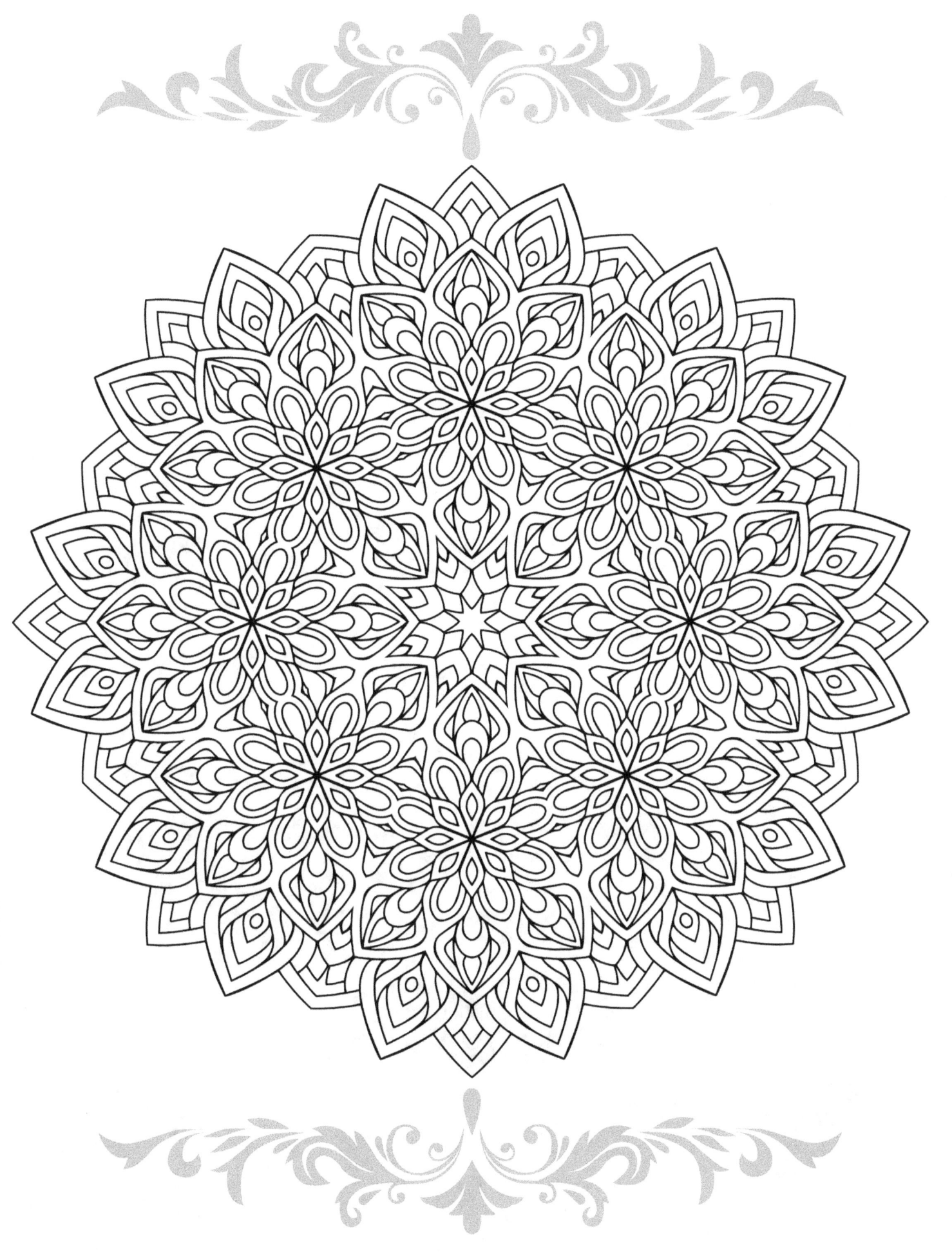

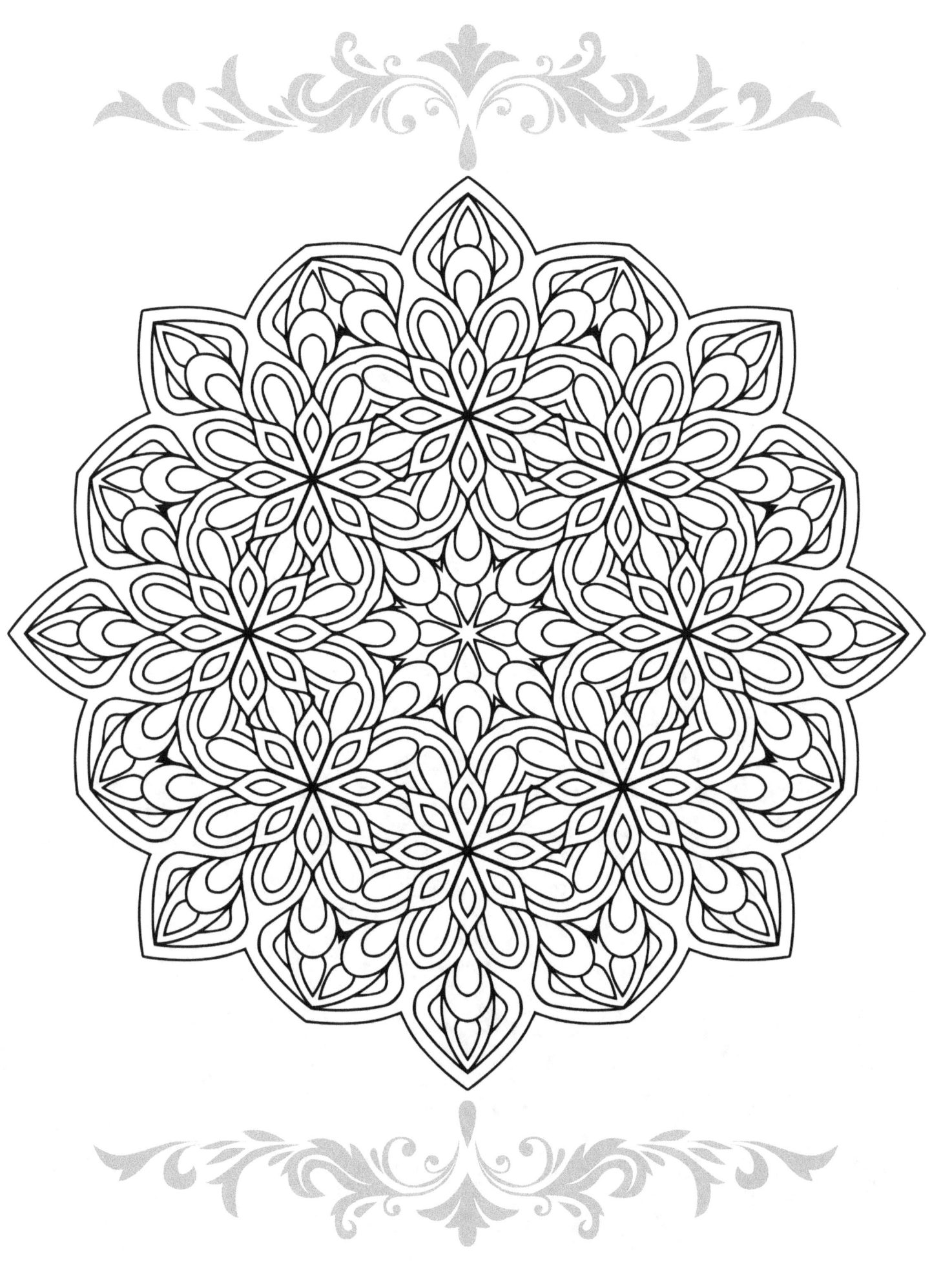

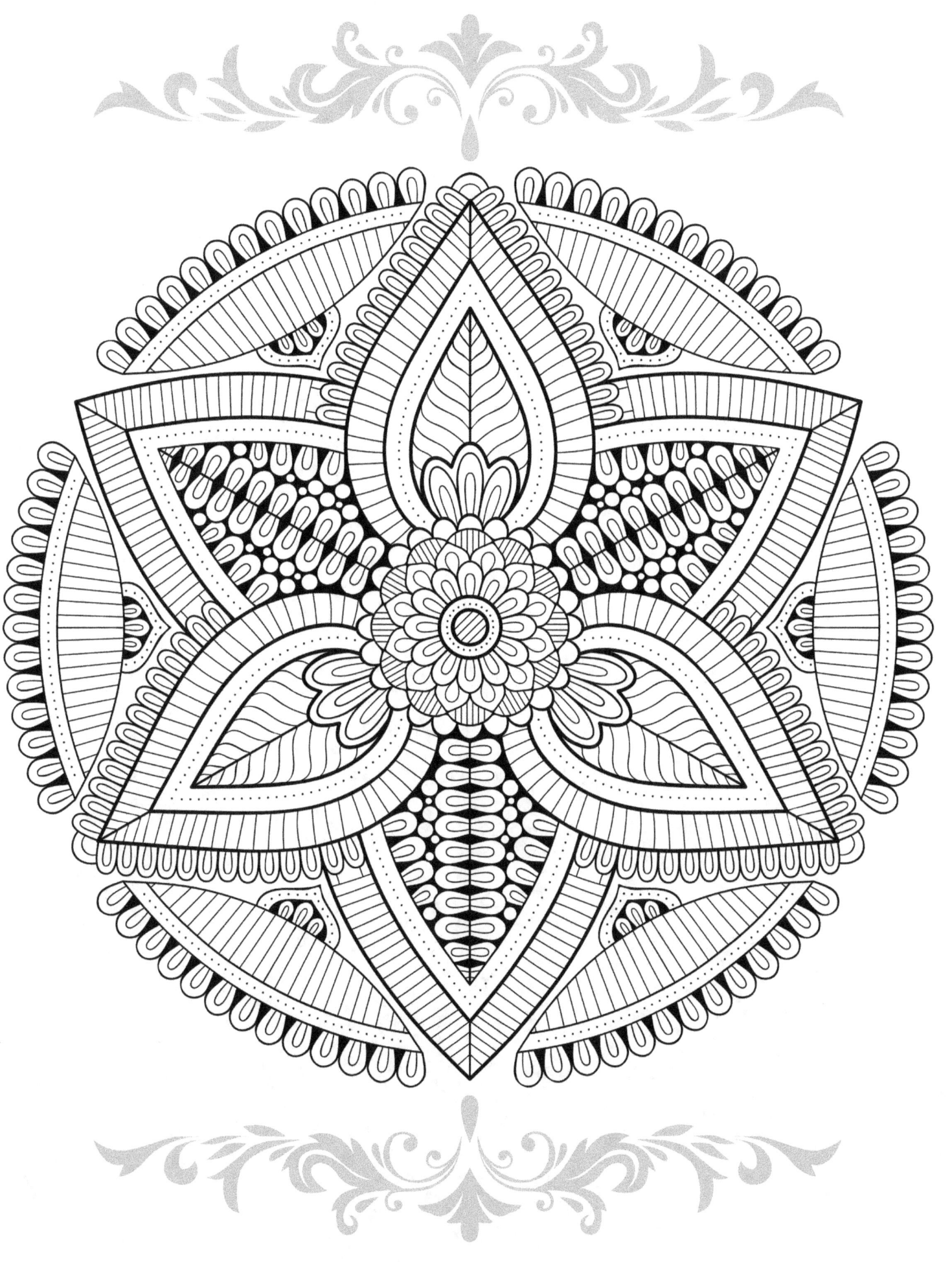

Thank You

www.ingramcontent.com/pod-product-compliance
Lightning Source LLC
Chambersburg PA
CBHW08083820526

45467CB00008B/2323

* 9 7 9 8 7 0 7 1 1 8 2 6 5 *